LAND OF THE CHIMAERA

LAND OF THE CHIMAERA

*An Archaeological Excursion in
the South-West of Turkey*

SYBILLE HAYNES

1974
CHATTO & WINDUS
LONDON

Published by
Chatto & Windus Ltd
42 William IV Street
London WC2N 4DF

*

Clarke, Irwin & Co Ltd
Toronto

ISBN 0 7011 2005 3
© Sybille Haynes 1974
Printed in Great Britain by
Fletcher & Son Ltd Norwich

FOR DENYS

CONTENTS

CONTENTS

ILLUSTRATIONS

Endpapers

Colour plates

ACKNOWLEDGEMENTS

For photographs and permission to reproduce them I am greatly indebted to the German Archaeological Institute, Istanbul (pp. 100, 108, 111, 113), to Dr. Herbert Cahn, Basle (p. 105) and to the Conservateur-en-Chef of the Cabinet des Médailles, Paris (p. 76).

I am grateful to the Trustees of the British Museum for permission to reproduce the photographs on pp. 22, 24, 31, 32, 33, 41, 45, 52, 64, 65, 67, 68, 69, 70, 71, 72, 73, 78, 79, 80, 81, 82, 85, 87a, 103 and on the endpapers and the jacket.

The following photographs were taken by D. E. L. Haynes: pp. 14, 16, 20, 26, 28, 36, 38, 48, 54, 55, 60, 62, 63, 74, 87b, 89, 91, 99, 102, 109, 114, 121, 124, 125, 127, 130, 133, 135, 140, 144, 147, Colour Pll. 1, 2, 3, 4.

FOREWORD

πρόσθε λέων, ὄπιθεν δὲ δράκων, μέσση δὲ χίμαιρα

'A LION in front, a snake behind, and in between a goat.' Such was the shape of the monster Chimaera, according to the 6th Book of the *Iliad*. Among the mythical exploits of the hero Bellerophon in Lycia, the most famous was his slaying of this three-headed, fire-breathing creature. But, although he killed the beast, its name and image continued to haunt the south-western extremity of Asia Minor, where the eight rocky capes of Mount Cragus are washed by the Mediterranean Sea. Some seven centuries after Homer, Strabo, the Greek geographer, wrote: 'It is to these mountains that the fables related of the Chimaera are applied, and in the vicinity there is a ravine called Chimaera, opening to the sea.'

This remote part of Turkey had captured my imagination from childhood, when bed-time reading used to be Greek mythology rather than fairy-tales. Later, years of work in the British Museum brought a close familiarity with monuments and sculptures which originally came from classical sites in Caria and Lycia; and the desire to follow in the tracks of the 19th-century travellers and scholars who had visited these regions and brought back the antiquities grew irresistible.

When my husband and I first visited Turkey by car in 1961, the extreme south-west was only accessible to motorists by jeep; and we did not get beyond Didyma in those days. Ten years later we returned to find communications much improved, and we were able to visit the fabled land of the Chimaera in an ordinary small car.

This book is an account of our journey southward from Didyma. Though it covers many of the important archaeological places of south-west Turkey, it does not attempt to be a comprehensive survey, or to compete with scholarly publications or straightforward guide-books. It is essentially a personal chronicle of an immensely enjoyable month, but I hope it may yet provide useful historical, archaeological and practical information for intending travellers in these parts.

Fortified island in Lake Bafa

I

HERACLEIA UNDER LATMUS

Bɛş Parmak Dağ—Five Finger Mountain—is the Turkish name for the serrated crest of Mount Latmus, which dominates the south-east confines of the vast coastal plain of the river Maeander. This wild range of granite crags had beckoned us into Caria on previous visits to Priene and Miletus; not least because, tucked under its boulder-strewn flanks at the eastern end of Lake Bafa (Bafa Gölü) lie the remains of the ancient city of Heracleia. Ten years ago, Heracleia was almost inaccessible except by boat. Now it is easily reached by car, and we decided to make it the first halt on our way south.

Originally it was called Latmus, like the mountain towering behind it; and it was not until the 4th century B.C., after its capture by Mausolus of Caria, that it was renamed Heracleia. In antiquity Lake Bafa was part of the sea and known as Latmikos Kolpos, the Latmian Gulf. But the restless alluvial activity of the Maeander gradually silted up the deeply indented bay, and Heracleia, like its more powerful western neighbour Miletus, became land-locked. Originally a harbour-town which prospered on sea-born trade, Heracleia still had an anchorage in the 1st century B.C. But when this inlet of the Aegean finally became a lake and the city was cut off from the sea, a decline in prosperity inevitably set in, for which there was no fertile hinter-land to compensate.

In early medieval times, the cave-riddled crags of Mount Latmus became the refuge of hermits driven from their desert homes in Egypt and Syria by the Arab conquest; and the 8th and 9th centuries saw a flourishing com-munity of monasteries, strongly fortified against Saracen raiders, grow up on the slopes of the mountain and on the islands of the lake. But the advance of the Seljuks into Asia Minor was a direct threat to the existence of the anchorites and monks around Heracleia, and in 1079 abbot Christodoulos left the Latmus to found the monastery of Saint John on the island of Patmos. Despite a precarious revival of the Christian communities in the 12th and 13th centuries, Islam had asserted its rule throughout western Asia Minor by the early 14th century, and the frescoed churches and grottoes of remote Latmus fell into ruin and were forgotten.

The remains of the ancient city were first visited by the Dilettanti Society's expedition to Asia Minor in 1764, and in the early years of this century the site was systematically explored by German archaeologists whose discoveries

The tomb of an Islamic saint

revealed Heracleia as one of the most beautiful of all ancient cities. We caught our first glimpse of Lake Bafa, silver-blue beneath the shadow-streaked flanks of Mount Latmus, from the airy terrace of the German dig-house in Akköy, which overlooks a magnificent panorama of the Maeander valley.

Turning east from Akköy to join the new asphalt road to Milâs, we overtook lumbering peasants' carts, their sloping sides constructed of wooden slats interwoven with green branches or lined with black goat-hair blankets. On a stony patch by the road-side an old man threshed his corn by driving over it on a wooden sledge, studded underneath with blades of flints and drawn by two horses. An occasional whiff of D.D.T. reached us from the alluvial plain of the Maeander. For centuries a fever-ridden swamp, the land has been drained in recent years and now produces large crops of cotton. But resistant strains of anopheles mosquitoes have already developed and a certain amount of malaria has returned to the villages.

Before long we left the plain behind, and the road began winding among low hills, sparsely dotted with pines, in whose shade a few black nomad tents were pitched. As the road descends again towards the southern shore of Lake Bafa, the vegetation grows much lusher. Here ancient olives and pines cover the steep slopes. Presently a white-washed tomb came into view on the left under a gnarled old olive. A green turban wrapped round the top of the head-stone proclaimed it to be the tomb of an Islamic saint. The tree is a çaputlu ağac—a tree of rags—for its branches are hung with white and coloured rags, mementoes of the pilgrims who have visited the tomb.

In the village of Bafa a track leads off to the left through cultivated fields, where minute, tower-like houses are almost choked by a profusion of fruit-trees, vines, sweet-corn and tobacco. Pumps chug away at the way-side, irrigat-ing a paradisiacal valley. The contrast between this fertile little plain and the strange view at the sandy eastern end of the lake almost makes one doubt one's eyes. From the towering flanks of Latmus on the right enormous blocks of granite, displaced during some primeval seismic upheaval, tumble down like a gigantic avalanche.

Here at the north-eastern corner of the lake the foothills of Latmus form a promontory, its outline echoed a little way beyond by a small, rocky island. In antiquity the island was connected with the shore by the walls of Hera-cleia, whose beautifully regular ashlar masonry of local stone is preserved in long stretches dominated by square towers. The circuit with internal subdivisions, for strategic reasons, enclosed not only the city, which was planned on a regular grid-pattern, but also large parts of the uninhabited mountain-side. Isolated forts and watch-towers perched on desolate outcrops of rock high up the slope give the impression that the city was much larger than in fact it was.

No inscription or other external evidence has survived to tell us the date when the fortifications were built. An attractive suggestion makes Mausolus, the Hellenized ruler of Caria, responsible for their construction, when he annexed Heracleia in the second quarter of the 4th century B.C. But the German excavators inclined towards a later date, about 300 B.C., when, in the aftermath of Alexander's death, Heracleia and its territory passed into the possession of Pleistarchus, the brother of Cassander of Macedonia, and formed a buffer state between the territories of Alexander's successors, Lysimachus and Seleucus. Whatever the precise date of the defences, their creator was a genius with an eye for beauty as well as strategic advantage. The elegance and strength with which the walls wind and climb up the rocky scarp is astonishing. In places where the stones of collapsed stretches have entirely disappeared, the cuttings in the living rock for the lowest course of masonry are clearly visible, ascending the mountain-side like a flight of stairs for super-human beings.

When the midday glare begins to dissolve the serrated crest of Latmus into an insubstantial silhouette, it becomes easy to imagine the goddess of the moon, Selene, descending from these luminous crags to kiss the sleeping mortal Endymion, whom myth associated with these parts.

A sanctuary of the hero Endymion has, in fact, been identified in the lower part of the ancient town, just above the present day track leading to the village of Kapıkırı, on a steep bank among olives and oak scrub. The sanctuary differs from most Greek temples in facing south-west, and it is also of unusual shape. The deep porch consists of five unfluted columns between square pillars of greyish local stone. Behind it the chamber, which once had a pair of internal columns, ends in a semicircular apse, formed partly by huge granite rocks left in their natural state and partly by masonry. The building must originally have been roofed, perhaps with large stone slabs, as was the enigmatic, grotto-like sanctuary in the side of Mount Cynthus on the island of Delos. Both shrines give one an impression of deliberate primitiveness and were probably built in the Hellenistic period as romantic recreations of an earlier, more rustic age.

The modern village of Kapıkırı has grown up with the ruins of the elevated northern part of the city, where most of the public buildings of Heracleia were situated. Of the ancient council-chamber all that survives is traces of stepped seats running round three sides of the square interior and a couple of column drums, overgrown by weeds and olive saplings. Some way beyond to the north-east lie scanty remains of a theatre and a fountain house.

To the west the large level expanse of the ancient agora now serves as a playground for the village-school. The southern edge of this market-square is bordered by a well-preserved, two-storeyed building divided into shops. The beautiful walls of this market-hall are a typical example of the high quality of civic architecture of the Hellenistic period.

Further to the west, lifted against the sky on a rocky pinnacle, stands the temple of Athena. The temple chamber is preserved to its full height, but of the columns, which originally stood in front of it, little survives. In spite of its rather austere, box-like appearance, the temple cannot fail to impress by its incomparable position and the beauty of its masonry. The dedication to Athena is recorded in a handsome but fragmentary Greek inscription to the left of the entrance.

Far below the temple and separated from the mainland by a shallow stretch of calm water lies the small island once included in the city-fortifications. Traces of the stepped cuttings for the foundations of the original walls can still be seen at the northern end. The island is now occupied by the ruins of a crenellated Byzantine fortress, whose poorly constructed walls incorporate classical column drums and pieces of Doric entablature.

A more extensive Byzantine fortress straddles a spur of the city walls, which defended the promontory forming the southernmost part of the town. Its crumbling gates and windows, hemmed in by ilex and oak, look down on to steep declivities falling away to the water and honeycombed with deep rectangular hollows carved in the bed-rock: the sarcophagi of 'the Carians of barbaric speech' as Homer called them. The lids are mostly displaced and lie scattered about. Here, as elsewhere in these regions, the coastline has sunk and the lowest tombs are now submerged, darkly wavering shadows beneath the lake's surface which is burnished to silver by the midday breeze.

Further out in the lake, to the west, appears another island, low and wooded and incrusted with the ruins of yet more Byzantine monasteries; and beyond it the rocky outlines of the hills descend towards the Maeander valley, shrouded in the heat-haze.

2

EUROMUS

NEXT morning we continued south from Lake Bafa along the main Milâs road. After winding up through wooded hill-country, where tall Aleppo pines shine in the early sun, bright green against the darker firs, the road descends into a fertile plain. Our first goal was Euromus, a Carian city occupying the northern reaches of this valley and closely associated with Mylasa, the modern Milâs.

The site of Euromus lies a short distance south of the small village of Selimiye where remains of walls and column drums, overgrown by brambles, flank the road on the left. Beyond them, in the deep shade of a short side valley some 200 yards to the south-east, stands the weathered, greyish colonnade of the Temple of Zeus. Fortunately, as a large tent under the olive trees proclaimed, a party of Turkish archaeologists was working on the temple at the time of our visit, and Dr Serdaroğlu generously showed us round.

The temple is among the better preserved of those in Asia Minor, where most of the ancient sanctuaries have been thrown down by earthquakes. Of the Corinthian colonnade, which originally had six columns on the short side and eleven on the long, sixteen still stand and carry parts of the architrave. The slim shafts of a number of them are unfluted, as the temple was never finished. Tablets with dedicatory inscriptions are carved on many of the columns, recording that they were the gifts of individual magistrates and citizens.

Of the temple chamber only the foundations, three statue-bases and the tall, monolithic door-jambs which gave access to it are still in their original position. But a fair quantity of fine ashlar blocks of the walls lie scattered about within the colonnade, and our Turkish friends told us that they hoped to restore the fabric of the temple as far as possible with the surviving stones.

Sadly, much has disappeared for ever. When, in 1764, Richard Chandler, the leader of the Dilettanti Society's first expedition, visited Euromus (which he wrongly identified as Labraynda) and inspected the temple, he deplored that 'its marbles have been melted away, as it were piecemeal, in the furnaces for making lime, which are still in use by the ruin'. The need of lime for building and white-washing village houses accounts for the disappearance of innumerable ancient marble buildings all over the Mediterranean area.

The temple of Zeus at Euromus

The Turkish excavators are not only doing their best to consolidate the remains of the temple of Euromus, but their investigations have thrown fresh light on its history. The present building dates from the 2nd century A.D., but replaced an earlier one of the Hellenistic period. An inscription found while clearing the foundations of the platform refers to Zeus Lepsynus, a non-Greek epithet which shows that Zeus inherited the sanctuary of an older local god.

At the east end of the platform a large square altar and two bases have been unearthed, their fresh, reddish-white marble colour contrasts strongly with the sombre, weathered grey of the temple itself. They are contemporary with the Hellenistic temple.

Even earlier remains have recently come to light at the north-west end of the building: archaic terracotta slabs decorated in relief with chariots, partridges and floral scrolls, perhaps from an architectural frieze, as well as a number of votive figures.

The town of Euromus lies a little to the north of the temple. None of its buildings, among which a theatre, a ruined colonnade market square and baths can be identified, has yet been excavated. Olive trees and pines cover the whole area within the walls, which date from the Hellenistic period. A massive semicircular tower of fine ashlar blocks rises above the trees on a slope not far from the temple, its workmanship reminiscent of the walls of Heracleia.

The town's necropolis extended in the plain to the south-west of the temple. Numerous Carian tombs are to be seen flanking the path which leads from the temple to the main road and in the adjacent fields. They are partly cut from the bed-rock, partly constructed underground and covered with huge stone slabs. Plundered in antiquity, and now choked with rubble and weeds, they still await excavation.

3

MILÂS—MYLASA

MILÂS, the ancient Mylasa, the most important of the few towns in Caria, lies some seven miles from Euromus at the northern edge of a fertile basin ringed by hills. According to Greek tradition, the Carians were immigrants in western Asia Minor, having come originally from the islands of the Aegean. The Carians themselves, however, maintained that they were an indigenous people and related to the Mysians and Lydians.

The Carians seem to have lived mainly in small hill-top settlements and pastoral hamlets. Remote from the centre of Persian rule, to which they had been subjected from the middle of the 6th century B.C., they enjoyed a certain amount of autonomy under native princes, approved by the Great King. The earliest known of these local tyrants was Oliatus, who held power at Mylasa about 500 B.C. But the most famous Mylasan dynasty was that of the Hecatomnids in the 4th century B.C. whose ascendancy brought about far-reaching changes in Caria.

Hyssaldomus, Hecatomnus and Mausolus were able rulers and skilful politicians and, though nominally satraps of the Persian king, made themselves virtually independent. When Mausolus, the most remarkable member of the dynasty, succeeded his father in 377 B.C., he deliberately and ruthlessly Hellenized Caria. After greatly enlarging his territory, he transferred his capital from Mylasa to the Greek harbour town of Halicarnassus, which he rebuilt on an ambitious scale. Nevertheless, Mylasa remained an important city, and, with the neighbouring sanctuary of Labraynda, which Mausolus and his brother Idrieus endowed with splendid new buildings, it continued to be the religious focus of Caria.

As Mylasa has been uninterruptedly inhabited since antiquity, only scanty traces of the many temples for which it was famous have survived. They include part of the podium and a single Corinthian column of a temple which may have been that of Zeus Carius. The temple of Augustus and Roma, for example, which the travellers Spon and Wheler saw when they visited Milâs in 1675, had already been pulled down and used as building material for a mosque before 1765, when Chandler, Revett and Pars looked for it in vain. But two monuments of the Roman period, of which Pars made charming water-colour sketches now in the British Museum, are well preserved.

The first is a gateway in the north-eastern part of the town, which dates

The ancient gate-way at Milâs. Water-colour drawing by W. Pars

from the 1st century B.C. and is known as Baltalı Kapı, the Gate of the Axe, from the double-axe carved on the key-stone of the arch. The axe was a symbol of Zeus Labrayndus, a Carian deity represented on Mylasan coins as a warrior-god with axe and spear. He was the main divinity worshipped at the sanctuary of Labraynda, a place-name which is thought to be connected with the word labrys, double-axe. The sanctuary was situated in thickly wooded

hill-country to the north of the town and the gate may have marked the beginning of the paved Sacred Way leading to it.

The other ancient monument of Milâs to survive intact is an attractive
tomb on the southern slopes of Hıdırlık Hill to the west of the town, an area
used as a cemetery in Hellenistic and Roman times. The building is known
locally as Gümüşkesen, the Silver Pouch, and rises on a dusty little eminence

Funerary monument at Milâs. Water-colour drawing by W. Pars

between a couple of cypresses. It is modelled on the Mausoleum of Halicarnassus, the infinitely grander and richer temple-tomb of Mausolus. Only the
foundations of the Mausoleum have survived, but Roman writers have left us
descriptions of the building, from which it is clear that the more modest tomb
at Milâs copies its main features fairly faithfully.

The actual tomb chamber is situated in a tall, square base of fine masonry,
accessible through a door at ground level. Massive pillars in its interior sup-

port the floor of the upper storey, which was pierced by a hole through which libations could be poured from above. An open colonnade—two Corinthian double-columns between square corner pilasters on each side—forms the second storey, which may have contained statues of the deceased. The building is crowned by a now damaged shallow pyramid of five courses of decreasing size, each consisting of four stone slabs laid diagonally across the corners of the course below. The underside of the pyramid, visible from

The han at Milâs

the ground, is richly carved with geometric and floral patterns, originally picked out in colour.

The area of the former necropolis around the Gümüşkesen has recently been taken over by squatters, known as 'gecekondu', who arrive from the poorer rural districts and construct shelters overnight. According to an ancient law, the local authorities may not order them to pull down their improvised dwellings again, if they have succeeded in putting a roof on them before the next morning; once that has been done the newcomers are able to improve their quarters at their leisure. The children of the gecekondu thronged around us as we inspected the tomb, offering us hastily collected flowers in return for sweets.

In search of lunch we made our way into the centre of the town, where the steep alley-ways of the bazaar were pleasantly cool and sheltered by bowers of vines. Mahmud's restaurant, a spacious hall decorated by a local master with still-life and landscape paintings in the manner of the Douanier Rousseau, provided us with a delicious vegetarian meal, the butchers of Milâs being on strike.

Market-day had crowded the town with farmers and labourers from the surrounding countryside. In a square overlooked by a mosque and an old han or inn, different kinds of grain and sweetcorn, ranging from pale buff to vivid orange, were heaped on cloths on the ground.

The cobbled courtyard of the han was filled with the peasants' mules and donkeys, their patiently hanging heads seeking a narrowing strip of shade. Stairs led up to the semi-darkness of a rickety wooden gallery running round the four sides of the courtyard and backed by small dark rooms for travellers. An old weaver had set up his primitive wooden loom here, producing a handsome rough goats' hair stuff—black with thin white stripes—which his boy-assistant made up into saddle-bags on the spot and sold to the farmers. Nothing much can have changed in this inn since Chandler and his companions stayed at Milâs over 200 years ago.

4

BODRUM—HALICARNASSUS

SOUTH of Milâs the indented peninsula of Halicarnassus stretches west-wards, its wooded hills and ridges dotted with the ruins of innumerable ancient settlements and small towns which were once the habitations of the Lelegians. The origin of the Lelegians is obscure. Herodotus and Strabo claim that they were of the same race as the Carians, but Homer mentions them as a distinct people settled in the southern Troad. According to Strabo, they founded eight cities in the neighbourhood of Dorian Halicarnassus. Apart from Myndus and Syangela, all the cities were abandoned in the 4th century B.C., when Mausolus transplanted their inhabitants to enlarge his newly adopted capital of Halicarnassus.

These inaccessible, deserted Lelegian sites have recently been investigated by Dr W. Radt, a young German archaeologist, who has published plans of hamlets, citadels, farm-houses and stone-built, corbel-vaulted tombs. Although the winding, modern road must pass close to some of them, we could not see a single one of the overgrown Lelegian settlements from the car. The only buildings occasionally visible on the dry hillside were brilliantly white-washed Turkish reservoirs. Circular in plan, with shallow vaulted domes and low entrances, their construction curiously resembles that of the Lelegian tombs described by Dr Radt.

As we climbed higher through the pine forests, we frequently noticed trees with their trunks gashed at the foot in a herring-bone pattern for the extrac-tion of resin, the tangy scent of which filled the air. Before long we began to catch glimpses of the sea, and soon the forest gave way to olive groves and cultivated slopes descending towards the port of Bodrum, the ancient Hali-carnassus.

The Roman architect Vitruvius, who must himself have visited Halicarnas-sus, speaks of the city as having the 'curved shape of a theatre', a singularly apt description, if one imagines the circular, almost enclosed harbour as the orchestra of an ancient theatre, and the gradually rising slopes embracing it as the auditorium. But none of the buildings mentioned by Vitruvius has sur-vived, and the modern town, though it preserves the shape of its predecessor, consists of small Turkish houses and shops, white-washed and red-roofed among trees, with a couple of mosques and some pleasant little hotels and restaurants on the quay.

On the peninsula which forms the eastern arc of the harbour rises the huge mass of the Castle of St Peter, built by the Knights of St John in the 15th century. This easily defensible site was no doubt chosen by the first Dorian inhabitants and has remained a citadel throughout the centuries.

The waterfront sweeps in a circle from the castle in the east to a promontory in the west which was formerly occupied by the Turkish arsenal. Within the arsenal's crumbling walls a shipyard still operates, as it probably has for thousands of years.

Beyond the little headland of the arsenal lies a pebbly beach under a steep bluff of rock, on top of which sections of the walls in which Mausolus enclosed his new capital are still preserved. Somewhere in this neighbourhood the fountain Salmacis must have been located, infamous in antiquity for the emasculating effect of its waters.

To the south, on the far side of the Bay of Bodrum, stretches the sombre ridge of Karaada—the Black Island—and beyond it the shadowy contour of the Cnidian peninsula reaches westwards towards the island of Cos. Herodotus, 'the father of history', who was born at Halicarnassus in the first half of the 5th century B.C., must often have recalled this view when in exile at Samos or in retirement in distant Thurii in South Italy.

Here, in his native city, one can get an inkling of the complex background which moulded Herodotus' perceptive and tolerant mind; and it is perhaps no accident that an intellectual advance of such importance as the rise of historical writing should have occurred in the coastal regions of Asia Minor, where mainland, sea and islands are linked in a way which invites travel and interchange of ideas, and where the mixture of different races and systems of government flourishing side by side must have provided a powerful stimulus for the development of a sense of history.

Bodrum from Gök Tepe

5

THE MAUSOLEUM

THE word Bodrum means subterranean vault or dungeon in Turkish; and was presumably first applied to the place by the Turkish invaders, who must have found substructions and upstanding parts of many ancient buildings still in existence.

The most famous monument of Halicarnassus was the tomb erected for Mausolus about 353 B.C. by Artemisia who was both his wife and his sister. The Mausoleum, as it was called, was one of the Seven Wonders of the World and its name has become a synonym for a stately sepulchre. From ancient writers we know that it was a rectangular building standing on a tall base and surrounded by a colonnade of 36 Ionic columns, which supported a stepped pyramid crowned by a four-horse chariot-group. The total height of the monument was about 42 metres. Its architects were Pytheos and Satyros, and four famous Greek sculptors were employed to carve its sculptural decoration: Leochares, Bryaxis, Scopas and Timotheos.

Vitruvius tells us that the Mausoleum was situated on a broad platform in the centre of what he describes as the auditorium of the hillside, and half-way up its slope; a dominant position which must have already been reserved for it when Mausolus' new city was first laid out. It seems probable therefore that it was originally intended to be not merely Mausolus' tomb, but a memorial for the whole Hecatomnid dynasty.

The Mausoleum apparently survived more or less intact until the 13th century when it was thrown down by an earthquake; and the destruction was completed by the Knights of St John who used it as a quarry when they enlarged their castle at the beginning of the 16th century. Its location was thereafter forgotten; but in 1749 the traveller Richard Dalton succeeded in gaining admission to the castle, which was by then a Turkish fortress. He discovered built into its walls a number of relief-slabs from a frieze which, he suggested, must have come from the Mausoleum. In 1846 Sir Stratford Canning, the British Ambassador at Constantinople, obtained the Sultan's permission to remove thirteen of these slabs which he gave to the British Museum.

The arrival of the sculptures in London made a profound impression, particularly on a young assistant in the Department of Antiquities at the British Museum, C. T. Newton, who determined to find the site of the Mausoleum.

But it was not until 1857 that his dream was realized. The intervening years, spent in the consular service, had given him the opportunity to excavate in the Aegean islands and to visit Bodrum. Exploration of Halicarnassus, however, started only in 1856, when various spots in the town, suggested by earlier scholars as likely locations for the Mausoleum, were unsuccessfully sounded. In January 1857 Newton decided to investigate a site which in his view corresponded better with Vitruvius' description. It lay about 150 yards to the north of the Aga's Konak, a former residence of the local governor, and was entirely covered with small houses and gardens.

Almost immediately he came upon rock-cut foundations for a huge building and a mass of fragmentary marble sculptures, some of which matched in size and style the reliefs which had been immured in the castle: he was convinced that he had found Mausolus' tomb. Further excavation resulted in the discovery of a large number of original Greek sculptures of outstanding quality and beauty, which are now preserved in the British Museum.

Among the most impressive are the over life-size marble statues of a draped man and woman and part of a gigantic marble horse, which Newton found shattered into many pieces in a position which suggested that they had fallen from a great height. It has been proposed that all three sculptures belonged to the four-horse chariot group which surmounted the tomb, and that the male figure with its strikingly individual features is Mausolus himself and the female Artemisia. Mausolus' hair falling in thick tresses down to his shoulders and his moustache and closely-cropped beard characterize him as non-Greek. The noble, brooding face with its wide brows and deep-set eyes expresses immense energy, tempered by intelligence. It is also one of the earliest true portraits to have come down to us—a portrait we can recognize as the likeness of a particular person, not a representation of an idealized type.

The face of Artemisia—a draped and veiled figure of corresponding size—is unfortunately missing; only her formalized Persian coiffure has survived. A number of other fragmentary statues, including a fine figure of a rider on a prancing horse, wear Persian dress, another reminder that the sculptures, though purely Greek in style, were commissioned by a patron who owed at least nominal allegiance to an oriental empire. These figures are probably portraits of other members of the Hecatomnid family and of Persian dignitaries.

The sculptural decoration of the Mausoleum also included three friezes which represented respectively battles between Greeks and Amazons, battles between Lapiths and Centaurs, and a chariot race. The Amazonomachy frieze seems to have run round the tall base of the tomb—an unusual arrangement also found in Lycian architecture, from which the architects of the Mausoleum probably borrowed it. The Centauromachy perhaps adorned the upper part of the tomb, while the chariot frieze, though very fragmentary, shows little

A marble horse from the chariot group of the Mausoleum

Marble statues of 'Artemisia' and 'Mausolus'

weathering and must have come from some sheltered position either within the colonnade or even in the interior of the building. The subject may have a funerary significance, since games, including chariot races, formed part of the ancient burial ritual.

The great divergences of style which can be observed in the Amazonomachy frieze lend weight to the tradition that each of the four sculptors employed by Artemisia was responsible for a different side of the Mausoleum. Each master would, of course, have had a number of assistants.

Of the palace of Mausolus, which was built of brick and marble, nothing has survived, and its precise location is in doubt. It must, however, have been situated somewhere near the isthmus which divides the main harbour from the shallower bay to the east of the Castle peninsula. For we know that

Battle of Greeks and Amazons. Slab of a marble frieze from the Mausoleum

Mausolus constructed a secret harbour next to his residence, and that this secret harbour was connected with the great harbour by an artificial canal. It was with ships hidden in this secret port that in 352 B.C. the newly widowed Artemisia surprised and overcame a Rhodian fleet after it had actually sailed into the main harbour, confident that it would have no difficulty in wresting Caria from a mere woman. To punish the Rhodians' presumption and to humiliate them the victorious queen set up a trophy on the island of Rhodes which showed her in the act of branding her enemies' city.

This self-glorification of a ruler anticipates Hellenistic practice; and the Hecatomnids foreshadowed later developments in other ways, notably by adopting for dynastic reasons the old Pharaonic custom of marriage between brothers and sisters, which was to become the norm for the Ptolemies of Egypt. In their foundation and transplantation of cities, in their ceaseless building activity, and in the attraction of poets and artists to their court, Mausolus and Artemisia set the example for the rulers of the Hellenistic world.

The site of the Mausoleum, which we approached by a cobbled village street leading north from the main harbour at a point not far from the quay-side mosque, lies inconspicuously among modest houses and walled gardens. Newton would still feel at home here: the sepia photographs, taken during his dig over a hundred years ago, show the same small cubic houses built of rubble and shaded by olive and fig trees.

While we were looking down into trenches where beautiful stretches of the great marble precinct-wall of the Mausoleum, its rock-cut foundations and some earlier tombs have recently been re-excavated by a Danish expedition, the owner of one of the cottages invited us to inspect her home. The immaculately clean interior was divided into a kitchen-and-living-area at ground level with an open hearth and a long divan, while the bedroom was no more than a mat-covered raised space. Here frugal nomadic habits have survived and there are no bedsteads; but the bedding is stored in a cupboard by day and unrolled on the floor at night. The owner—a pleasant, fair-haired woman in her forties, who wore trousers, dress and headscarf of faded, flower-print cotton—allowed us to take a picture of her house, but superstitiously shrank from being photographed herself.

We crossed the barren open space left by the last excavators, where a few forlorn-looking column drums and blocks of masonry are all that now survives of Mausolus' tomb, and climbed up the flank of Gök Tepe, the scrub-covered, rocky hill which dominates Bodrum on the north-west.

Half-way up the slope lie the remains of the theatre of Halicarnassus. The stage building has disappeared completely, but the semicircle of the auditorium is preserved in the hillside and disjointed rows of seats lie scattered about in the sparse shade of Vallonia oaks and olives.

In the perpendicular rock-face crowning Gök Tepe above the theatre are the dark caverns of Carian rock-tombs. After clambering up to them, we found these roughly carved chambers with benches running round three sides much defaced and smoke-blackened from centuries of use by shepherds and their flocks. The arched entrance of one of the tombs framed a splendid view of the glittering bay and the castle, which stood out white and shapely against the mauve ridge of Karaada and the paler distant chain of the Cnidian peninsula.

The summit of Gök Tepe, the 'Hill of the Sky', was enclosed within Mausolus' great city walls. A level platform on top of the hill suggests that a temple was once situated here, but no trace of a building survives.

6

THE CASTLE OF BODRUM

THE Castle of St Peter, whose construction caused the ultimate disappearance of the Mausoleum, is now, by contrast, dedicated to the preservation of antiquity. The vast complex of fosse, courtyards, chapel and towers, abandoned by the Knights in 1522 and subsequently used by the Turks as a fortress and prison, has been imaginatively restored as a museum.

The approach through the west fosse, flanked by walls emblazoned with the Knights' coats-of-arms, is lined by ancient sarcophagi, tombstones, altars and weather-beaten sculpture. Other marbles are displayed on the upper terraces, between the former chapel and the buildings clustering round the French and Italian towers, where agavae, hibiscus and bougainvillaea soften the dazzling glare of the crenellated fortress walls.

The existing buildings have been pleasantly adapted to make small, self-contained museums, each devoted to a different theme. The fascinating Under-water Museum houses finds brought up from the bottom of the sea, which range in date from the Bronze Age to Medieval times. Here are the contents of a Syrian merchant ship wrecked about 1200 B.C. off Cape Chelidonia in Lycia and raised in 1960 by archaeologists from the Pennsylvania University Museum. The cargo, which probably came from Cyprus, consisted of quantities of copper and bronze ingots cast in the shape of ox-hides—the raw material of a travelling bronze-worker's shop, whose tools and products are also partly preserved.

A later Greek shipwreck yielded a charming bronze figure of a young negro boy; and a remarkably varied range of household utensils and portable pottery stoves was brought up from a sunken Byzantine vessel.

There are primitive stone anchors and crumbling iron ones, the latter encased in thick layers of marine incrustation, which has preserved their shape. Many of these finds are casual ones, made by local sponge divers, but the most spectacular and informative exhibits are those retrieved by systematic underwater exploration and restored by expert conservation methods.

The Carian Museum contains the discoveries made in the neighbourhood of Bodrum and in southern Caria. In recent years Turkish scholars have thrown fresh light on the earliest history of the region. A number of Mycenaean vases have been found at Müsgebi, to the west of Bodrum; and Geometric vases and a terracotta sarcophagus found at Dirmil and dating from the 9th and 8th centuries are tangible evidence of the Dorian colonization recorded by ancient historians.

Among the finest objects in the museum is a slab from the Amazon-frieze of the Mausoleum, which was found in 1964 built into the wall of the west fosse of the Castle. It shows a Greek treading on the hip of a collapsing Amazon, whose head he is pulling back by her helmet. The violence implicit in the action is mitigated by the beauty of the movement of the Greek's naked body, balanced against the blank background with the elegance of a dancer. This relief completes a run of three consecutive slabs excavated by Newton on the east side of the Mausoleum; and its recent discovery strikingly illustrates the vicissitudes suffered by the sculptures, and suggest the exciting possibility that the Castle walls may conceal further surprises.

A Museum of local Islamic Antiquities is planned. In the Director's office we were shown a collection of Turkish metalwork, including chased copper ewers, dishes, candlesticks and camel-bells, waiting to be exhibited.

The highest part of the Castle is on the east side, a rocky plateau surrounded by walls and towers, which had turned into a crucible in the midday heat. We climbed to the top of the circular 'Snake Tower' and looked down on the entire town with its two bays spread out before us in a blaze of light. In the main harbour close to the isthmus, massive rectangular foundations of ancient moles can be made out, shimmering through the clear aquamarine water—they have been thought to be the substructions of Mausolus' secret harbour, but this, as we have seen, more probably lay on the east side of the isthmus, where now the town's second ship-yard is operating.

We crossed the scorching inner bailey to the ruinous English Tower, splendidly situated above the rock-bound southern tip of the peninsula. Its restoration is planned but has not yet been put in hand; and the numerous inscriptions and heraldic emblems of the English Knights, incrusting the walls of the oblong interior, are sadly exposed to weathering.

The main harbour of Bodrum from the castle

7

CROSSING THE CERAMIC GULF

To reach Cnidus by boat from Bodrum takes three to five hours, depending on the force of the imbat, the wind from the sea which prevails in the Aegean during the summer. We had agreed with the captain of a motor-caïque to start our trip before dawn on the next day.

Under a night-sky alive with stars we made our way to the boat at four o'clock. At this early hour only the slightest of breezes rustled in the palm trees on the waterfront, planted by the poet Cevat Şakir, the 'Fisherman of Halicarnassus', during his exile.

Not a soul was to be seen on the quay, where small yachts and sturdy caïques were silently lying side by side under the looming mass of the castle. A stray dog slunk past; several cats brushed along the moon-lit walls of the harbour-mosque and from the distance came the first cock crow. Presently the muezzin arrived on a bicycle, climbed to the top of a minaret and sang out the call to morning-prayer.

A faint streak of dawn outlined the hills in the east and the stars began to pale. It was by now five o'clock, and a small party of American and Italian tourists, who had contracted to share our caïque, straggled along the quay and joined our vigil. Their leader eventually managed to rouse a cabin-boy and sent him off in search of our tardy captain. Meanwhile the muezzin had descended from the minaret and pedalled along the waterfront to the next mosque, from which his call shortly came across the dark water. Suddenly the eastern horizon was touched by pink, and with the waxing light a fresh wind sprang up, which whipped the calm expanse of the harbour basin into a cauldron of choppy waves: the imbat had arrived before our crew.

At last the captain made his appearance; but no sooner had he done so than he returned home for the ship's papers; after which the boy was sent out for bread and water, and lastly the captain's dog had to be persuaded to go ashore. Whining and shivering pitifully it was finally ejected and we cast off.

Having wedged ourselves between the mast and some low railings on top of the cabin, where the strong roll of the boat was least noticeable, we gazed at a landscape constantly transformed by the increasing light and the progress of the caïque. The sky behind the sombre silhouette of the Lelegian hills became suffused by a brilliant orange. With startling suddenness a sheaf of

The two harbours of Cnidus

firey shafts shot upwards in the east and the disc of the sun, huge and blinding, soared above the rampart of wooded mountains. Like innumerable shattered mirrors, the facets of the deep petrol-blue water foaming past us caught and reflected the light.

The richly indented coastline of the Bodrum peninsula to the north glowed in a luminous mauve, while the Carian hills to the south were bathed in melting shades of honey and hazy gold. Behind us, still trapped in dim shadows, the rapidly receding castle and harbour of Bodrum had become almost invisible until the sun was high enough to release them, too, into colour and life.

Ahead in the south-west lies Cos, its bleached ridges softening into a wide green plain on the landward side. A small Greek steamer passed us on its way there. Though no longer a centre of medical teaching and cure as in the days of Hippocrates, the island nowadays attracts the more discerning Greek holiday-maker by its Theocritean beauty and its ancient ruins.

Our caïque made good speed; within three hours we had crossed the Ceramic Gulf, and Cape Crio, the westernmost point of the Cnidian peninsula, heaved above us, lashed by a fierce land-wind, the meltem. This rocky outcrop was originally an island, but the gap between it and the mainland had already been artificially reduced in antiquity to form a narrow channel spanned by a bridge. It is now an isthmus.

The wind-swept headland, on which a lighthouse now stands, was understandably feared by ancient sailors, but the choice of two good harbours compensated them for the dangers in approaching Cnidus. Our boat fought its way round the tip of the promontory and made for the calmer waters of the southern harbour.

8

CNIDUS

CNIDUS belonged to the Dorian Hexapolis, a league of the southernmost Greek settlements along the west coast of Asia Minor, which, at first, included the cities of Lindos, Ialysos and Camirus on Rhodes, the island of Cos and Halicarnassus. The members met periodically to celebrate the festival of Triopian Apollo in the territory of Cnidus. But Halicarnassus was expelled from the league when one of her victors in the games flouted the custom of dedicating the prize bronze tripod in the sanctuary of Apollo and kept the trophy for himself. Henceforth Cnidus was the only remaining mainland member of the Dorian league, now named the Pentapolis.

Because of its geographical position Cnidus always had better communications with the Greek islands and mainland and with the west than with Anatolia from which it was separated by a long, narrow and mountainous peninsula. In the early 6th century B.C. Cnidian colonists settled briefly on the north coast of Sicily, but were driven out by the local inhabitants and moved on to new homes on Lipari. Cnidian dedications in the sanctuary of Apollo at Delphi where they had a treasury and a splendid assembly room, decorated with frescoes by the famous painter Polygnotus in the 5th century B.C., show that the citizens frequently consulted the oracle and were often victorious in the Pythian games. When the Persians undertook the conquest of the coastal Greek cities of Asia Minor after 546 B.C., the Cnidians attempted to turn their peninsula into a defensible island by cutting through the narrow neck of land at its easternmost end. But they suffered so many casualties from splintering rocks that they sent for advice to the Delphic oracle which recommended them to desist; and they surrendered to the Persians without a struggle.

Cnidus was famed in antiquity for its wines, its vinegar and its olive oil, which were all exported widely. But it was more renowned still for its intellectual achievements and artistic patronage. It gave birth to scientists and architects, among them Eudoxus, the 4th-century mathematician and legislator, who discovered the star Canopus; the historian Ctesias, who became physician to the Persian king Artaxerxes Memnon; and Sostratus, who in the 3rd century B.C. built the Pharos, or Lighthouse of Alexandria, which was one of the Seven Wonders of the World. Sostratus also built a 'Pensilis ambulatio', or hanging walk at Cnidus, a construction which has been plausibly recognized in a large colonnaded portico in the Doric style, recently excavated on an elevated terrace in the western part of the city. Another important new discovery is that of the round temple of Aphrodite Euploia (protectress of sea-faring) which housed Praxiteles' marble image of the naked Goddess of Love, the most famous statue of the ancient world. It was situated high up in the north-western corner of the city, overlooking the harbour.

Cnidus was explored by the Society of Dilettanti in 1812 and subsequently partly excavated by C. T. Newton in 1857/8. Since 1967 American archaeologists have been working on the site, identifying and clearing many of the buildings found by their predecessors which had collapsed or completely disappeared from sight, and making many new discoveries of their own.

It is a striking fact that none of the surviving architectural remains are earlier than the mid-fourth century B.C. Professors Bean and J. M. Cook have argued from this that archaic Cnidus was situated elsewhere and have recognized it in a site further to the east along the south coast of the peninsula near the modern village of Datca. But this view is disputed by the present excavators, who have suggested that archaic Cnidus should be sought on the as yet hardly explored south-eastern slopes of the headland of Cape Crio. In support of their theory they cite a number of pottery sherds, bronze fibulae, an unfinished archaic statue of marble and fragmentary terracottas of 6th and 5th century B.C. date which have turned up in the current explorations; only further excavation can finally decide this important question. What is certain, however, is that sometime about the middle of the 4th century B.C. the Cnidians rebuilt their city on the present site.

It was obviously chosen for the possibility it offered of creating two harbours between Cape Crio and the mainland: the smaller 'Trireme harbour', which faces north-west towards Cos, and the larger commercial harbour, which faces south-east towards Rhodes. Communication between the two basins was provided by a channel (now silted up) which pierced the massive artificial causeway by which Cape Crio was linked to the mainland. Two moles laid in deep water protected the commercial harbour: huge blocks of the western one still emerge above the surface, but all that can be seen of the eastern one are its submarine foundations clearly visible in calm weather.

The terraced slopes of the ancient city face each other across the wide harbour basin. Laid out on a regular grid-pattern, the streets and stairways on the eastern, mainland side are oriented roughly north–south and east–west, and most of the public buildings of the town were located on this slope. The rocky declivities of the promontory of Cape Crio seem to have been given over to quarters composed of private dwellings, which were differently aligned. Well-built walls of ashlar and polygonal masonry, reinforced by towers, protected both parts of the city. On the northern, landward side the

*Marble statue of the
goddess Demeter from Cnidus*

wall ran along the elongated crest of a steep limestone ridge dominating the town, on the easternmost summit of which was situated the acropolis.

Apart from the lighthouse and a few low, white-washed buildings on the pinkish pebbly beach between the two harbours, no modern buildings exist at Cnidus. The rising, terraced ground, streaked with sparse bands of scrub and meagre fields, shows numerous fresh scars where excavations have been carried out. As we arrived we could make out an army of workmen—ants at this distance—busily engaged in digging a site high up in the north-western corner of the city. From the cascading spoils of the dig the fierce wind raised clouds of dust, blurring the outlines of the scene. So little of Cnidus is now preserved above ground that, at first sight from the boat, it looked a little disappointing, a tree-less slope criss-crossed by trenches.

While we dropped anchor and tied up to the small modern landing-stage, we were met by Miss Iris Love, the American archaeologist directing the excavations.

Originally our plan had been to gain a general impression of the site and to take photographs to illustrate the provenance of the sculptures brought back to the British Museum by Denys' distinguished predecessor Newton. But Miss Love offered to take us on a conducted tour of her numerous excavations in the town.

Preceded by her dachshunds, she guided us over the glaring slopes, through a maze of old and new trenches and partly cleared classical ruins, frequently incrusted with the remains of Byzantine churches. In their brief report on Cnidus the Dilettanti mission scathingly referred to such buildings as 'rubbish of the time of the Byzantine empire', a view not shared by modern excavators who rightly treat these more recent remains with as much respect as earlier ones since, apart from their intrinsic artistic merit, they often incorporate re-used stones bearing Greek inscriptions, or carved architectural fragments, which help to throw light on preceding buildings.

Such was the case with the Christian church (Church C) situated to the west of the harbour-side theatre. It was built in the 5th century A.D. on top of, and using materials from, a large Ionic temple, already identified in the 19th century as a temple of Dionysus on the strength of its proximity to the theatre. Temples of this god, to whom wine and dramatic art were sacred, were frequently associated with theatres.

The harbour-side theatre has been investigated by the present excavators, who found that the cavea, or auditorium, was built in the Hellenistic period and modified at a later date. The existing stage-building seems to have been constructed in Roman times to provide a raised stage floor and an elaborate decorative architectural façade, the scaenae frons, behind it.

This was not the Cnidians' only theatre. A second and larger one was situated high up under the acropolis ridge; but it was almost completely dismantled when, about the middle of the last century, several shiploads of stones from Cnidus were removed to Egypt by order of Mehmet Ali for the construction of a new palace.

Climbing up past the foundations of the vast Doric portico, which has been ingeniously identified as the famous 'hanging walk' of Sostratus, we reached a terrace immediately above it. Here stood once a handsome small Corinthian temple which was seen and drawn by the Dilettanti and partly excavated by Newton. Built of marble, it was raised on a high podium on a stepped base and had four columns on the façade and six engaged half-columns on each long side. It is now a heap of ruins. When the American archaeologists explored it recently, they discovered the central blocks of the pediments, which were decorated with large raised shields. The temple dates from the 2nd century A.D. Nearby was found a sun-dial, marked with the seasons as well as the hours.

On our way up to the highest, westernmost terraces of the city we passed the remains of a Roman odeum or hall for musical and poetry recitals, situated a little to the west of the Corinthian temple; some of the stepped semicircular rows of seats are still preserved. The Cnidians seem to have held music and poetry in high regard, for there are the ruins of a second odeum in the south-eastern part of the town, overlooking the commercial harbour near the point where the great eastern breakwater projected from the shore.

Still higher up above the first odeum and to the north-west of it are the remains of the round temple which Miss Love has convincingly identified as that of Aphrodite Euploia. It occupied a spectacular position close under the northern city wall and commanded a view over both harbours. Surrounded by 18 Doric columns, it stood on a stepped base accessible from the east, on which side there was an altar. Although the present building dates from a later period than the mid-4th century B.C., when Praxiteles carved the famous figure of the naked goddess, it evidently replaced an earlier shrine which originally housed the image. In all probability the later temple is that referred to in Pseudo-Lucian's 'Love Affairs', a work of the 2nd century A.D., which describes it as standing in a sacred enclosure abounding in fruit-bearing trees. Next to the round temple a building which may have served as a treasury has been excavated, and beyond it an altar and a dedicatory inscription to the goddess Athena. A cave in the rocks nearby contained numerous votive gifts including terracotta lamps.

This lofty and exposed spot is still 'fanned by breezes', and the view from it on this windy day was exceptionally clear. Beyond the dazzling white lighthouse of Cape Crio, the long, scoured spine of Cos and the islands of Telos and Nisyros appeared as if etched by a firm hand on the translucent horizon; and southwards, across the Gulf of Syme, the distant pinkish silhouette of Rhodes seemed to be afloat.

On a terrace below the temple a large number of Turkish workmen were

moving a vast amount of earth. Here, among the extensive ruins of a rectangular building which may have been a congregation hall, fragments of
marble drapery and of a hand have turned up, which, Miss Love hopes, will
prove to have belonged to Praxiteles' statue. The search for further fragments
is obviously keen. Adjoining the hall lies an altar adorned with a figured
frieze. In this area sacred performances probably took place, since the site is
dominated by rows of theatre-like stone seats ranged on the slope above it.

On our way down to the 'Trireme harbour' we passed the western end
of the stubble-covered terrace on which Newton spent the exceptionally
severe winter of 1857/8 in an encampment of wooden huts of the type used
in the Crimean War. The threat of jackals, wolves and pirates proved less
of a trial to the expedition than the penetrating northerly blast which
swept the site for weeks on end.

To the west of the terrace the foundations of a temple have recently been
uncovered which, according to a dedicatory inscription found on its podium,
was sacred to Apollo Karneios; the inscription honoured C. Julius Artemi-
dorus, son of Theopompus, the Cnidian friend of Julius Caesar, who tried in
vain to warn him of the Ides of March.

North-east of the 'Trireme harbour' a small Byzantine church (Church 'D')
had been partially excavated. Straddling a late Hellenistic building, it was
composed of stones taken from the earlier structure, which included unusual
corner pillars with a Doric half-column engaged to each of the two inner
faces. A series of 13 curved marble slabs with Greek inscriptions, which must
originally have formed part of an exedra or semicircular monument, was
skilfully adapted by the Christian builders to form the apse. These inscriptions
refer again to honours paid by the Demos of Cnidus to Theopompus and
his family.

We returned to the American dig-house after only a cursory glance at
the harbour which Strabo refers to as the 'Trireme harbour'. It could ac-
commodate as many as 20 warships, and a chain across its mouth, which was
defended by towers, made any assault on it hazardous. Remains of steps, store-
rooms and handsome stretches of walls can still be made out under tufts of
mastic and myrtle.

Our hostess kindly insisted on our sharing an open-air lunch with her and
her team. The geese of the lighthouse keeper waddled up to the table from
the beach, honking demandingly and clearly used to participating in meals.
'They are the geese of Aphrodite,' we were told, while they were being fed.

In the heat of the early afternoon the glassy water of the main harbour
had become a mirror reflecting the fierce rays of the sun and the glare from
the torrid, tree-less slopes. A little dazed by the intensity of light and heat, we
climbed into a broiling Land-Rover, which was to take us to the foot of the
ascent to the sanctuary of Demeter. But before we reached that dark cliff
brooding above the city, we were shown an insula, or block of private dwell-

Marble lion from the Lion Tomb near Cnidus

ings near the eastern confines of the town; a stepped street with landings
borders it on one side. Overlooking the harbour-basin, this complex of
terraced, super-imposed houses dates from the Hellenistic and Roman periods.
Interesting and colourful remains of a wall-decoration of moulded and
painted stucco turned up in a Hellenistic house. Pieces of a Doric, an Ionic
and a Corinthian order imitated in stucco were found, as well as numerous
fragments of painted plaster dados, feigned marble veneer and panels with
genre and mythological scenes, all once united in a rich decorative scheme.

A Roman house with an open colonnade was later constructed on the slope
above the Hellenistic building, making use of part of it. Spacious and comfortable, these private houses were supplied with water and drainage and faced
a delightful prospect of sea, rocky promontories and distant islands; this must
have been among the most enchanting residential quarters of the ancient
world.

When we had finally tackled the rugged ascent to the temenos, or sacred enclosure of Demeter, the afternoon was well advanced. While Miss Love was taking photographs of some trenches recently opened on the western side of the sanctuary-terrace, we were able to take in the extent of the excavation carried out in this inaccessible spot by Newton during the summer of 1858. He cleared the entire ground within the walled precinct to a considerable depth, a labour which produced not only a beautiful statue of the seated goddess Demeter, but also a prodigious mass of fragmentary sculpture almost exclusively related to the cult of the gods of the Underworld.

Among them was the marble head of a young woman which Miss Love claims to be the head of Praxiteles' famous statue of Aphrodite, unrecognized, unpublished and long neglected by the British Museum. But we know from Roman copies of the Cnidian Aphrodite what she looked like, and the British Museum head certainly differs from hers in at least one very important respect. The roughly worked surface of the sides of the neck and at the back and on top of the British Museum head prove conclusively that it was originally veiled, whereas the beautifully dressed hair of the Cnidian was uncovered and the whole of her neck was visible. The British Museum head most probably belonged to a draped statue of Kore, the daughter of Demeter, in whose sanctuary it was actually discovered.

In the smooth face of the cliff towering at the back of the terrace are carved four irregularly spaced rectangular niches: they may have contained votive figures, but they are now empty and situated strangely high above the ground level, which has been much disturbed and lowered by the excavation. An oppressive stillness pervaded the stunted trees and scattered boulders under the dark rock-face here, and we turned to the edge of the terrace to look out over the Gulf of Syme glittering in the evening sun.

In the middle distance the rocky promontory of the Lion Tomb reaches southwards into the sea. We had hoped to visit it, too, as it was the site of one of Newton's most spectacular finds. It was here that he came upon the ruins of a monumental tomb of the Hellenistic period modelled on the Mausoleum and originally crowned by the gigantic marble figure of a recumbent lion, which was lying on the ground and which he brought away with great difficulty. But any lingering hopes we may have had of getting there were now extinguished by distant but repeated hooting from the 'gazino', the little resturant by the landing-stage, where our crew had been feasting and now wished to remind us that our caïque had no lights, and that we must leave in good time to get back to Bodrum before nightfall. Distressed that we had seen so little of the town and nothing of the vast necropolis to the east of it, Miss Love urged us to stay on, but the peremptory claxon summoned us back to the boat.

While we collected our belongings in the dig-house, we were shown a marble block recently found near the round temple. It bore a fragmentary

Greek inscription including the first four letters of the name Praxiteles and the first three of Aphrodite.

Two of our fellow-passengers of the morning were staying behind to help clear up the excavation, which was nearing its end for the season. We said good-bye to them, competing with the strains of Parsifal blaring out from a dusty record-player; but when we looked for our hostess to thank her properly, she had disappeared mysteriously. Our apolaustic crew had some difficulty in getting up the anchor and there was a short delay. When we finally got away, an out-board motor-boat raced after us pulling behind it a waving figure on water-skis: it was Miss Love circling our caïque to bid us farewell.

9

FROM CARIA INTO LYCIA

WE were on our way south once more. But to reach the road to Muğla and Fethiye, we had to return from Bodrum to Milâs. On the somewhat dreary plain between Karaova and Güllük we were held up by Nomad children, who blocked the road with outstretched arms and urgent shouts of 'gazete! gazete!' Newspapers are in great demand—not as reading matter, but to light fires with and for other practical uses.

The narrow, undulating road made overtaking impossible. We remained for some time in the dusty wake of a tractor pulling an open trailer full of girls and women—country-folk, going to some feast. At first we only saw their back and heads covered with squares of spotless white woollen cloth. When they noticed us and turned around, the girls' brilliant emerald and purple dresses were revealed, and bright sashes knotted at the side of the head. Two of them held coloured parasols over babies cradled in their laps. Sparkling eyes smiled, shyly at first, then with open enjoyment, and we exchanged waves.

Climbing up from the Milâs plain, green with tidy patterns of fruit and olive plantations, into the pine-covered hills to the south, the road became a shifting mass of gravel, built up on either side in embankments, narrowing or widening the passage according to the fancy of the last earth-moving bull-dozer. It was hard on our tyres. Soon, too, the car was covered, inside and out, with a pinkish-white fur of dust, as was the vegetation bordering the road for a depth of several yards. At intervals great excavating machines, like monstrous orange elephants, were stabled in the shade by the roadside.

We passed through sparsely-inhabited hill-country and reached the village of Eskihissar which nestles within the scanty ruins of the Hellenistic city of Stratoniceia. From the road only a few ancient walls and column drums were visible among the trees, but there is a small local museum in the modern settlement, which was entirely rebuilt after a devastating earthquake in 1958.

Shortly before Muğla we joined the great road from Aydın, the main north–south route, which is already asphalted as far as Muğla. The town, one of the seats of the emirs of Menteşe during the 15th century, now possesses only a few old buildings. Leaning against a hill which faces west, the town's upper part still follows the contours of the landscape with small white-washed, wooden-roofed houses of pleasant proportions, while the lower part is already inorganically shapeless with harsh concrete blocks of flats and offices. In one of these modern buildings the 'Zebek' restaurant provided us with an excellent luncheon, and its friendly waiter guided us to the bazaar, where an acquaintance of his, an optician, mended Denys' sun-glasses, refusing to charge for this service.

From the brown, harvested fields surrounding Muğla, we reached rugged uplands, dominated by stately pines. On top of a pass, where we stopped to clean a thick layer of dust off the windscreen, we caught an enchanting glimpse of immense forests sloping down towards an azure inlet of the sea, the innermost corner of the Ceramic Gulf. Far in the south-east, the towering pyramid of Sandras Dağ, the first of the barren Lycian peaks, was visible, softened by the gentle golden afternoon light.

The air was droning with millions of bees. Their strange hives—hollow sections of tree-trunks, piled in a heap, topped by rush-matting and weighed down with stones—were massed everywhere under the trees. Carian pine honey was to be the most delectable part of our breakfast for the next week.

Later in the afternoon we crossed the marshy plain bordering Lake Köyceğiz. In the west, beyond the calm, silvery sheet of water, rise low humps of green hillocks among which hide the ruins of ancient Caunus, infamous for its unhealthy climate. Its walled acropolis, its theatre and its imposing rock-cut tombs have recently been explored by Turkish archaeologists.

Again we wound up into hills covered by extensive woods, the natural wealth of this region. Frequently we were forced on to the ill-defined margin of the road by timber-lorries, transporting bulky loads of reddish pine-trunks to the camps of the ormanci—the forestry workers. Their drivers were obviously not used to meeting private motorists and hugged the crest of the road with lordly disdain for the possible consequences of a head-on encounter.

Plunging down into a valley again, we crossed the Dalaman river, the ancient Indus, glittering in its wide bed of shingle. Then over yet another pass and so down with many a bend to a secretive inlet of the sea, rock-bound, overhung by trees and full of evening shadows. This region abounds in chromium mines; and further along the road we noticed the guarded entrance to a camp, where the ore, extracted from the mines in the Kizil Dağ, is processed for export.

Suddenly the frowning cliffs opened out, and we found ourselves as if on a balcony overhanging the bay of Fethiye, the ancient Lycian Telmessus. Low hills in the foreground already had the cool, blue look of approaching night. In the middle distance the pines on a higher ridge stood out, burnished like bronze as they caught the last light. The pale stretch of water beyond mirrored the sky, from which the colour was fast fading; but the distant chain of Massicytus in the east still kept its hyacinthine glow.

10

FETHIYE—TELMESSUS

Fethiye, the ancient Telmessus, was known as Makri until recent times, having taken this name in the Middle Ages from the island which lies, studded with Byzantine ruins, at the northern entrance of the bay. In antiquity this Gulf was called Glaukos Kolpos. Its sheltered inner harbour, its fertile coastal plain and its mountains rich in timber made Telmessus an attractive site for settlers from ancient times.

Some Mycenaean pottery has been found in the neighbourhood, illuminating the Homeric tradition of the Lycians' Greek descent: Glaukos and Sarpedon, the leaders of the Trojans' Lycian allies, traced their lineage from Argos and Crete. The names of the Lycians themselves was, according to Herodotus and others, owed to an Athenian—Lycus, the son of Pandion—who has sought refuge with Sarpedon and his Termilae, the people who subsequently took Lycus' name.

The surviving Lycian monuments of Telmessus date, however, not from this mythical past but from the 5th and 4th centuries B.C. and from the Roman period. The best preserved and most spectacular are the rock-carved tombs and sarcophagi situated in the vicinity of a conical outcrop of rock which rises from the alluvial plain, between the eastern shore of the bay and the sheer cliff-face of the westernmost mountain-bastions of Anticragus. This was the citadel of Telmessus, surrounded by a vast necropolis.

Of the public buildings of Telmessus little has survived. When, about 1781, Count Choiseul Gouffier came to Makri, as it was then still called, he found substantial monuments still extant, among them a great theatre of the Roman period. But time, the Ottomans' need for handy building material and earthquakes have dealt roughly with these antiquities. Benndorf and Niemann, the Austrian archaeologists who visited the town in 1881, found that the theatre had almost disappeared, its masonry having been used for the construction of barracks at Scutari. To-day the site of the ancient theatre only betrays itself by a hollow in the hillside, which was once the auditorium, and a semicircular piazza, the former orchestra, in front of it. The 'Yıldız Sineması', an open-air cinema, has installed itself on the curved slope as a modern successor to the older forms of entertainment patronized here by the citizens of Telmessus.

As we walked from our hotel at the far end of the town to the small museum which houses the local archaeological finds, we took in the extent to which Fethiye had been destroyed by the earthquake of 1958: it had to be almost completely rebuilt. The uncompromisingly modern reconstruction has created new quays and a massive mole, wide, tree-lined boulevards flanking the harbour, quarters of identical, red-roofed dwellings and public buildings of concrete. Small ancient houses have survived only on the lower slopes of the acropolis and in the valley between it and the mountains to the east.

Among the modern constructions of the lower town, engulfed by paving or asphalt, a number of tall Lycian sarcophagi are preserved, their stone bases and sculpted chests surmounted by characteristic ridge-roofs of ogival shape. Next to the Belediye, the town-hall, a splendid example carved with panels and friezes in low relief stands as a witness to the changes which have overtaken Telmessus. Originally this western part of the town must have been a necropolis; but, as in many other coastal regions of Asia Minor, the level of the ground has subsided over the centuries and the sea invaded these sunken parts. A water-colour drawing made by William Müller about 1843 and now in the British Museum, shows this same sarcophagus emerging from the shallow water of the bay. After the earthquake of 1958 a lot of

Lycian sarcophagus in the bay of Fethiye. Water-colour drawing by W. Müller

land was reclaimed from the sea for the construction of the new harbour and waterfront, and so the sarcophagus once more stands on dry land, though rising somewhat incongruously from a gap in the modern paving.

Lycian funerary beliefs demanded burial not underground, but in elevated tombs in the open air. The earliest examples date from the 6th and 5th centuries B.C. and take the form of a simple stone box, sometimes decorated with reliefs and roofed by projecting stone slabs, the whole structure raised on a tall, smooth pillar set on a base.

More elaborate examples reflect the timber construction of actual houses in their upper parts: a panelled framework with morticed joints and projecting beam-ends, covered by a ridge-roof, which has either a triangular pediment or, more normally, an ogival one, in which case the roof looks rather like a boat with its keel turned uppermost.

There can be no doubt that the domestic architecture of Lycia was chiefly wood-construction, as one would expect in a country so rich in forests; and in burying the dead in an imitation of the architecture used by the living, the intention was evidently to make him feel at home. But the house of the dead had to be of more durable material than wood.

Flat-roofed wooden houses, too, are imitated, mainly in the façades of rock-cut tombs: here the timber framework of the walls with its recessed panels is covered by slim, closely-packed tree-trunks laid horizontally, their round sections appearing as a row of circles above the façade. The roof above them seems to have been of beaten clay, confined between wooden fascias, which are faithfully reproduced in the stone imitation.

With the growing influence of Greek architecture the forms of Lycian tombs underwent a gradual Hellenization. The characteristic structural elements of carpentry disappeared, supplanted by Greek architectural forms. The upper part of the tomb was frequently modelled on the Ionic Greek temple with its columns, mouldings and friezes; and many rock-cut tombs of this type can still be seen in Lycia, including three well-preserved examples in Fethiye itself. Free-standing, masonry tombs of temple-form also existed, but were probably rare and in any case more exposed to damage by earthquakes and stone-robbers. Of the few which still stand the Nereid Monument at Xanthos is the earliest and most splendid.

After a visit to the modest local museum, we made our way to the tomb-riddled rock-face which towers above the modern town in the east. Here almost all the possible variations of tomb-façades are represented in the perpendicular grey cliff, from simple, rectangular panelled frame constructions to more elaborate schemes with two storeys, in which the triple fascia of the flat roof is no longer supported by the traditional row of round sections of tree-trunks, but by the dentil-frieze of the Ionic entablature.

The most striking façades in this part of the necropolis are, however, the three highest which are closely modelled on the Ionic 'templum in antis', a

Lycian rock-tombs under the acropolis of Telmessus

temple porch consisting of two Ionic columns framed between the projecting side walls or antae, and surmounted by the entablature and a triangular pediment. The acroteria, or decorative end-tiles which crown the gable and corners of the roof, are only roughly blocked out from the rock but details were once added in paint. Traces of paint were still preserved in the 19th century on the lintel of the doorway of the highest of the three tombs, that of Amyntas, so-called from the name 'Amyntou tou 'Ermagiou' (son of Hermagios), carved in Greek letters on the left anta.

All the features of a temple-portal, the panelling of the two-leafed door, the heads of the bronze nails with which the frames were studded, and the rosettes which decorated them, are here repeated in stone, and so give us a vivid idea of what the door of a Greek temple would have looked like. The small, square burial-chamber of the Tomb of Amyntas was accessible only through the right hand bottom panel of its mock-doorway, which was once closed by a sliding stone slab. Now there is only a gaping hole, since this tomb, like all the other tombs of Telmessus, has been broken into by tomb-robbers.

In the lowest of the three temple-tombs, the left-hand column of the façade has been partly broken away, leaving the capital and the upper end of the shaft suspended from the entablature like a stalactite.

As we were walking towards the acropolis, a small, dark girl with an intelligent, long face framed by pig-tails emerged from a crowd of children which had collected round us, and invited us into her parents' garden, where, she said, more tombs were to be seen. We followed her into a warren of small houses surrounded by fig and lemon trees, which covers the lower slopes of the acropolis hill on the north side. Here isolated outcrops of rock were sculpted

Ionic rock-tomb in the necropolis of Telmessus

into free-standing sarcophagi, against which the modest wooden huts lean in strange familiarity. A scantily-dressed ancient, who lived in a cottage below one of the sarcophagi, pointed with a skeletal arm to a funerary procession carved on the side of its chest—his daily memento mori.

Higher up the slope, just clear of the cluster of trees and cottages, stands a group of three rock-cut burial chambers, the pediment of the central one decorated with carved palmette-shaped acroteria; and on the landward side the lower part of the acropolis cliff is fretted by tomb-façades imitating timber-frame constructions.

The small girl, whose name was Melek—Angel, had already plundered a fig-tree for our benefit, and now insisted on guiding us up to the top of the acropolis; she seemed fascinated by visitors from a dazzling foreign world. Making sure at intervals that we were following her, she leapt ahead from boulder to boulder like a mountain-goat.

The summit of the hill is crowned by a fortress from which crumbling walls straggle downhill. On the parched slope, among tall thistles and mullein, we came upon the massive stone-jambs of a gate, the lintel of which, covered with a long, but illegibly weathered inscription, had been thrown down by an earthquake. The motley character of the existing masonry on the acropolis-hill suggests millennia of successive building activities by Lycians, Greeks, Romans, Byzantines, the Knights of St John and the Turks. On top of the citadel, mounted on a metal frame, is a maze of electric bulbs which, as we discovered in the evening, form the glowing outline of a gigantic male profile —that of the ubiquitous Atatürk.

We clambered over the shoulder of the acropolis-hill on the south to get an unobstructed view over the bay, a placid aquamarine in the sheltering embrace of the pinkish headland and of the island of Meğre Ada, dotted with pines. The fertile plain to the east with its dark green citrus plantations, smoky olive groves and flowering cotton fields contrasts strikingly with the barren mountain ranges behind. Hidden in remote valleys of these rocky chains lie the ruins of other Lycian cities—Cadyanda, Araxa, Oinoanda and Bubon—which are as yet little visited by tourists.

In the afternoon we set out to shop for a picnic for the following day. The bazaar is a clean, but characterless modern concrete square, where we brought bread and tomatoes and large red apples. For our evening meal we tried the 'Rafet' restaurant on the harbour which proved to be excellent and quiet; on the previous night—a Friday—we had been driven from it by the deafening rhythms of a jazz-band dressed in tails and white ties, an incongruous sight in this simple quay-side setting.

Two wide and heavy-bottomed Black Sea barges, painted an earthy red, were tied up at the mole beside huge stacks of timber waiting to be loaded; these handsome traditional vessels are still used for much of the Turkish coastal traffic.

II

THE XANTHOS VALLEY AND THE LETOÖN

EARLY next morning we filled up with petrol and bought a supply of bottled drinking-water. Good water and petrol stations are rare in the Xanthos valley.

From Fethiye we drove east, up-river, gradually winding higher into open forests of Vallonia oak and ancient pines. Every now and then large areas of the dark soil had been cleared of trees and planted with young olives. Bulldozers were still working on the edges of these new plantations, tugging at recalcitrant stumps and roots like exasperated terriers. Here the river had dwindled to a rill, and we soon reached the plateau which is the watershed between the Bay of Fethiye and the Xanthos valley. Through the dust raised by on-coming timber-lorries we began to make out the immense barrier of the Massicytus range, which flanks almost the entire length of the Xanthos on the east.

On reaching the western edge of the river-plain, we turned south to drive parallel with the course of the Xanthos, catching occasional distant glimpses of its shallow waters meandering in a wide bed of shingle and bordered by fields of maize, tobacco and cotton. Cotton-picking had already begun in this hot region: groups of women, up to their hips in an expanse of mottled green, rust and white, were busily bending over the crop. Their white head-scarves, wrapped so as to cover forehead, mouth and chin, are designed to protect the wearers from dust and strong sun; and the Persian soldiers on the 'Alexander sarcophagus' in Istanbul wear their head-dress in precisely the same way. In the harvested tobacco-fields the cut stalks had been set up in neat, tent-shaped stacks to dry; later on I noticed these withered stalks used for thatching cottages. Children grazing goats and cows on the lush hedge-rows waved and shouted gaily as we passed. Small, scattered farmhouses surrounded by pomegranates, figs and other fruit trees were bright with flowering plants grown in white-washed pots.

It is not surprising that this smiling, exceptionally fertile valley with its background of deep forests and craggy mountains, Homer's 'rich land of Lycia', was the setting of many ancient myths and fairy-tales—the wonderland where the monstrous Chimaera lurked in a ravine of rocky Cragus, the arena of the deeds of Bellerophon and the realm of god-like Sarpedon.

The west side of the Xanthos valley, where wooded spurs reach down from the barren bastions of Anticragus into open plains with scattered clumps of oaks, recalls an English park, though the strong southern light and the deep colours of the shadow-riven mountains suggests the Italianate landscapes of Claude and Poussin.

The age-old form of transport by camel and donkey still holds its own against the lorry in this region of rudimentary roads. While we were over-taking a camel-train at walking pace, the animals shied and broke out in different directions, sweeping their elderly owner off his donkey with the rope by which they were tied together. Before we could come to his help, he had calmly got up, dusted himself and remounted his splendidly embroidered saddle without deigning to look at us. His wife, meanwhile, had hastened up from the rear to restore order to the camel-train and readjust their loads, baled in fine, ancient kelim rugs.

Passing through a higher-lying hamlet with the suitably pastoral name of Çobanlar—the Shepherds—we noticed large patches of brilliant red on the carpet of needles under the pine-trees: they were the drying harvest of red peppers. The morticed beams of the storage-sheds nearby still preserved the tradition of ancient Lycian wooden construction.

Beyond the busy village of Eşen—until recently called Kestep—the forest closes in on the track again. Some scattered blocks of ancient masonry by the roadside are misleadingly identified by the Guide Bleu as the location of the Lycian town of Pinara, a site which lies, in fact, some miles further to the north-west among the rocky foot-hills of Anticragus.

A little further a bent sign-post, unexpected but helpful, pointed to the right for the Letoön. We wound down into open country of cotton-fields, bordered by scrub-covered hills—the last outposts of San Dağ or Cragus—which overlook the coastal plain of the Xanthos estuary. The track threaded its way across runnels of water shaded by poplars and mulberry trees. After crossing two small and shaky bridges we reached a plain among hillocks, where a few cottages crouch under fruit trees. On rising ground to the east stands the only substantial house of the hamlet of Kumluova and below it a çardak, or improvised pergola of brushwood and reeds, which shaded a table and chairs—the dig-house and al fresco dining-room of our French colleagues, the excavators of the Letoön.

We had hoped to find them at work, but the local guardian told us that the whole party had gone on an expedition to Pinara; so we set out to explore the site by ourselves.

The Letoön, or sacred precinct of the goddes Leto, was the federal sanctuary of the Lycian people. The place was first identified by Hoskyn in 1840/1, and has been systematically excavated by Professor Metzger since 1962. Because of the high water-table the site is particularly difficult to dig, and trenches once dry tend to refill with water, so that it is not always easy to make out the shape of buildings.

Clearly visible and most important are the remains of a group of three Hellenistic temples, which lie parallel to each other and oriented north–south on a dry terrace between two large flooded areas. The easternmost of these shrines was a Doric temple with an intricate plan. A fine floor-mosaic, composed of a bow and quiver, a large rosette and a lyre—the symbols of Apollo and Lycia—is preserved in the chamber and identifies the building as a temple of Leto's son, Apollo. On the slope near the east side of the temple a long tri-lingual inscription in Greek, Lycian and Aramaic dating from the 4th century B.C. has recently been excavated and will prove of the utmost importance for the final decipherment of the Lycian language. The text is of a religious nature and refers to Leto, her children and the nymphs.

The other two temples were Ionic. The larger was surrounded by a colonnade with six columns on the short sides; and quantities of marble blocks of its cella, colonnade, entablature and sima or gutter have survived. The sima is carved with palmettes and lions' heads. It is not known to whom the temple was dedicated.

The smaller Ionic temple in the centre seems to have been sacred to Apollo's sister, Artemis, whose name is given as Ertumi in an important Lycian inscription of the 4th century B.C. discovered near the building.

To the south-west of the temple-terrace the ruins of a nymphaeum or monumental fountain, with a central hall and a semicircular portico and a basin in front of it, can be made out in the turbid water which has again infiltrated the area drained during excavation. According to an inscription, the richly ornamented façade was built in the reign of the emperor Hadrian (A.D. 117–138). But earlier remains have been identified underneath the Roman structure and suggest that this sacred pool had a long previous history.

The whole flooded area is fringed by reeds and water-plants and pullulates with terrapins and small frogs—a perfect illustration of Ovid's tale of the marshy lake far down in the Lycian valley (*Metamorphoses* VI, 313 ff.). The poet tells how the wandering Leto with her infant children approached the lake to quench her thirst. But the inhospitable country folk who were gathering osiers by the bank shouted abuse at her and prevented her from drinking the water by jumping about in it, stirring up the soft soil from the bottom. Thereupon the enraged goddess punished their impiety by turning them all into frogs, which live, croaking forever, in the muddy pool.

To the east of the fountain and south of the temple terrace an Early Christian church with mosaic-floors has been uncovered. Here, as in many other ancient sanctuaries, the Christian builders seem to have chosen a site close to the heathen temples, not only with the intention of exorcizing the old divinities, but also, one suspects, in the hope of profiting from the continuing numen of the place.

We walked past the most recent excavation to the north of the temple terrace, where the high water-table covers the foundations of what appears to

Letoön. Entrance of the Hellenistic theatre

be a large Hellenistic portico enclosing the sanctuary. In front of it a number of inscribed stelae were found and, at a lower level, Lycian altars of the 6th and 5th centuries B.C.

Beyond the portico, leaning against the north-facing slope of a hill, a small Hellenistic theatre is almost engulfed by the luscious vegetation. In the beautiful masonry of the curved outside wall opens a dark tunnel framed by pilasters and a pediment, through which we penetrated into the cavea with its tumbled rows of seats. In the orchestra olive and fig trees flourish in soil washed down from the hill above. A corresponding arched passage leads into the theatre from the east side, its façade surmounted by a frieze in which triglyphs alternate with metopes decorated with sixteen theatrical masks. Large parts of the fabric of the theatre are so well preserved that it could be restored with comparatively little difficulty.

Beyond the dig-house, and out of sight, the French excavators have built a delightful little museum from local materials to house the finds made at the Letoön.

12

PINARA AND TLOS

THE path to Pinara which branches off the Xanthos road in a westerly direction is not distinguished by a sign-post, but in the distance the huge cliff of its acropolis appears above the pine forests and serves as a landmark.

Pinara means 'something round' in Lycian, a name no doubt inspired by the form of this tower-like bastion of rock which juts out from the curved escarpment of Anticragus. The abandoned ruins of the ancient town were discovered in 1840 by the English traveller Charles Fellows. Its name, modi- fied to Minara, survives in that of a small modern village which lies some miles below the classical site.

The track to Minara is more suitable for mules and Land-Rovers than for ordinary cars. It flanks one of the wooded ridges which Anticragus sends down into the Xanthos valley and, winding through a succession of small rock- bound plains, ends abruptly at the edge of the ravine in which the village nestles among thickets of daphne, styrax, olive and fruit trees.

We left the car in the cavernous shade of an old oak and were about to plunge into the green warren of the village, when a peasant introduced himself as the bekçi or guardian of the place. As we followed him up through the shady, narrow paths of Minara, which straggles along the western edge of the ravine, a youth offered us some indifferent Roman bronze coins, but slunk away when the bekçi reproved him. The village-elders who were smoking their pipes on a raised platform under the trees greeted us with formal dignity, while a group of women threading tobacco leaves in a garden nearby stole only side- long glances at the passing foreigners.

From the luxuriant vegetation of the ravine we emerged on to a tree-less shelf, where harvested fields stretched to the foot of a low, rocky ridge. Beyond it rose the spectacular, and now gigantic-looking, flat-topped cone of the acropolis-rock of Pinara, on the sloping summit of which the scanty remains of walls can be made out among broom and scrub. Isolated by two deep gorges from the main body of the mountain-chain behind, the acropolis is virtually impregnable. The precipitous reddish-grey flanks of this tower of rock are honeycombed by innumerable rectangular holes, the tombs of the earliest inhabitants who lived on top of it. The men who carved them must have been lowered from the top of the citadel on wooden cradles; and pre- sumably the dead were conveyed to their last resting-place in the same way.

The acropolis of Pinara

Continuing across the fields we rounded the south end of the ridge in the west face of which is the larger of Pinara's two theatres. The well-preserved auditorium, which is cut in the outcropping rock, follows the pattern of Greek theatres in exceeding a semicircle. It has twenty-seven rows of seats, subdivided by ten stairways. Of the free-standing stage-building, which was constructed of ashlar masonry, only the foundations and part of an entrance on the short south side survive. But the dramatic back-drop of the tomb-riddled acropolis, at the foot of which stretches the long, wooded terrace of the ancient town, more than compensates for the lack of an architectural stage-back.

From the topmost row of the seats where cyclamen push through the cracked soil, further groups of tombs can be made out flanking the town. They must date from a period when the acropolis was no longer used for habitation and burial but only as a refuge in time of war. To the south of the town, tombs with temple-like façades are visible in the deep shadow of a low cliff overhung by trees, while to the north a cluster of free-standing ogival sarcophagi, all but one tumbled from their tall bases, dominates a small plain. Passing the sarcophagi, on one of which we noticed a long Lycian inscription, we reached the pine-covered terrace where most of the public buildings of Pinara stood.

Despite the earthquake which evidently destroyed much of the town in early medieval times, Fellows was still able to recognize the remains of a

Rock-tomb at Pinara

number of buildings—temples, colonnades, a second theatre or odeum and cyclopean walls. But since his time the villagers of Minara have used them as a quarry and little is now to be seen but unintelligible jumbles of greyish masonry and rough column drums. Excavation may perhaps one day clarify the site.

Most of the local stone is a conglomerate, the rough surface of which does not take a high finish and is unsuitable for fine carving. T. Spratt and E. Forbes, who visited Pinara shortly after Fellows, saw tombs whose walls were coated with plaster scored to represent ashlar walls; inscriptions, too, were cut in the plastered surface of the tombs, the letters being picked out in blue and red or in yellow and green. Much of the now rough-looking stone may originally have been covered with smooth plaster.

From the site of the town we scrambled through thorny undergrowth on to a narrow ledge at the foot of a cliff-face overlooking the deep ravine which debouches southwards from the rear of the acropolis-rock. Here the most fascinating of the decorated tombs of Pinara are situated.

The first of these has a façade in the form of a house-front with an ogival roof. Since shepherds have used the interior as a shelter, the lower part of its frame of morticed posts and a double panelled entrance is badly damaged. But the mullions and transoms of the upper part are perfectly preserved and so are all the details of the wooden construction of a ridge-roof with curved sides. The most striking feature of the tomb is the pair of bull's horns and ears on top of the gable, a place where animals' skulls or antlers are still often fixed on actual houses to-day.

The other tomb, which is the largest of Pinara, lies further along the ledge. It, too, has suffered damage and is much blackened by herdsmen's fires, but its design illustrates an interesting transitional stage in Lycian architecture. The central post of the façade, which was modelled on the native open wooden porch, is unfortunately largely destroyed. Above the lintel a frieze of dentils or formalized rafter-ends and a shallow pediment reflect Ionic Greek influence. Of the low reliefs which decorated this upper part, hardly anything can now be made out. A horseman and dancing and sitting figures could still be recognized by Fellows. The fame of the tomb rests on two pairs of reliefs which cover the inner side-walls of the porch. Though much incrusted and stained by damp, they still show what appear to be four different views of a Lycian town in a mountainous landscape. The town is enclosed within crenellated walls with square towers and gates. Houses, some with the coffered façades familiar from the rock-tombs, cover the slopes, and on hills outside the walls groups of tomb-pillars and sarcophagi, just as we know them from actual Lycian cemeteries, are represented. On three of the reliefs human figures

Pinara. Rock-tomb with city-reliefs. Drawing by G. Scharf

The citadel of Tlos (the acropolis of Pinara in the background)
Water-colour drawing by W. Müller

appear—a man addressing two boys outside the walls, two figures in conversation in a small gate and a man standing beside a tall gate, his arm raised in greeting or prayer.

That this is the tomb of a local ruler anxious to immortalize his deeds is suggested by the analogy of the Nereid Monument at Xanthos, which bears similar representations of a city assaulted by an army. Though no actual battle is shown on the more modest reliefs at Pinara, we are surely meant to conclude that the city depicted here had been conquered by the owner of the tomb.

There must once have been other tombs with carved façades in this cliff-face, but violent earthquakes have dislodged whole portions of the mountain, and huge fragments of rock, in which length of carved entablature are visible, lie tumbled in the gorge below.

Looking out across the wild ravine and the wooded hills to the east, we caught glimpses of the Xanthos valley in the distance. Beyond it the immense barren crest of the Massicytus range rose, bleached as bone. Ak Dağ—White Mountain—is as fitting a name for it in the heat of late summer as it is during the rest of the year when snow covers its upper reaches.

At this point something of the remoteness of Pinara made itself felt and we decided to return to Minara without exploring the temple-tombs further to the south. We were thirsty, too, and the bekçi led us down the boulder-strewn gorge to a spring hidden among the roots of old plane-trees, where we drank from a gourd floating in the clear water. A gypsy-woman with her children was crouching in the green gloom by the pool, and our sudden appearance frightened her little girl, who buried her face in her mother's lap until we had gone.

On the way back to the village we followed the course of the water which rushes down over the rocks to the level terrace above the ravine of Minara, where it divides into various runnels to irrigate small fields. Under a carob tree we came upon a man with a gun and a party of boys armed with catapults; abandoning their bird-hunting, the boys followed us in a body. The bekçi walked stolidly ahead, while we trotted behind, dazed by the heat and almost mesmerized by the regular movement of the great patches on our guide's faded trousers and the flip-flop of his torn plastic shoes.

So we returned to Minara where the bekçi loaded us with grapes and tomatoes and we responded with a small bottle of eau-de-cologne, a gesture which brought a smile to his stern, wooden face for the first time.

The citadels of Pinara and Tlos, each magnificently sited on its hill-top, lie within sight of each other; but while the terrain of Pinara on the western side of the Xanthos was hilly and difficult to cultivate, Tlos dominated rich, open stretches of the river-plain, sheltered from the east by the unbroken rampart of the Massicytus range. The two cities must have been natural rivals for the possession of the central regions of the Xanthos valley which are among the most fertile in the whole of Lycia. But hardly anything is known about their history.

Like Pinara, Tlos was discovered by Fellows, who identified the town in 1838 with the help of inscriptions which he found on the spot. Although Tlos was visited by Spratt and Forbes in 1842 and by an Austrian expedition in 1881, no plan of the site has been published so far, and the place is not marked on ordinary maps of the region.

We found our way there by crossing the Xanthos at Kemer, a prosperous village on the Fethiye–Antalya road, and proceeding southwards along the east bank of the river as far as the village of Düver. Numerous small streams rushing down from the slopes of Ak Dağ ran across our track to join the Xanthos on our right, but as the road lies more or less at the same height as the river-bed, there was little inducement for the waters to drain, and we forded not only rivulet after rivulet, but large flooded stretches. In these clear, shallow pools cows stood contentedly browsing on hedges of pale lilac agnus castus.

Occasionally we passed through small villages occupying slight eminences which lift them just clear of the flood-water level. In two of these hamlets we noticed rustic wooden platforms constructed in the branches of huge plane

The monument of Izraza from Tlos. Plastercast in the British Museum

trees overhanging streams; these shady perches, cooled by the freshness of the water below, serve as meeting-places for the village-elders.

After a laborious drive of about an hour, we reached some farmhouses, where a track forked off from the river-bank in a south-easterly direction. It led through fields of sweet corn towards a huge outcrop of rock in the middle distance: the acropolis-hill of Tlos, outlined against the austere background of the Ak Dağ.

On the summit of the hill the walls of a Turkish fortress gleamed in the late afternoon light. Winding up towards the citadel along the crest of a rocky spur which approaches it from the north-west, we came upon a pinnacle of black rock rearing up on the left of the track. It turned out to be the monolithic base of a huge Lycian sarcophagus lying toppled on the slope below. This is in all probability the sarcophagus in whose vicinity, according to Spratt and Forbes, a square, stepped pedestal inscribed with the name Izraza and ornamented with reliefs of athletes, fighting warriors and the siege of a hill-town (perhaps Tlos itself) was once to be seen. Plaster-casts of these lively scenes were taken by Fellows in 1843 and are now in the British Museum. The badly damaged pedestal itself has recently been removed to the museum at Fethiye.

It was getting late when we stopped at the edge of a tree-filled ravine, the

Rock-tombs under the citadel of Tlos. Drawing by G. Scharf

opposite side of which was formed by the north-eastern flank of the acropolis of Tlos. Again, as at Pinara, this forbidding precipice served as the main necropolis of the town. But here the tombs carved into the rock-face are more elaborate than the simple oblong niches of the other city. The majority are of the type imitating flat-roofed, panelled wooden house-fronts, but the most important tomb takes the form of an Ionic Greek temple. Its columns are only roughly blocked out and the details of the capitals were probably originally painted. There are similar tombs at Fethiye, but this example is distinguished by having figured reliefs carved inside the porch. It is known as the 'Tomb of Bellerophon' from a relief representing the mythical hero on his winged horse Pegasus which is carved to the left of the simulated doorway leading from the porch into the actual tomb-chamber. When Fellows discovered this relief, it still bore traces of paint on the saddle-cloth. Facing the hero above the door-way appears a lion, not, as one might have expected, a Chimaera, for there is no trace of a goat's head in the middle of the back or of a snake's head at the end of the tail. The lion must be there not as Bellerophon's opponent, but as the guardian of the tomb, an old oriental motif.

The tomb of Bellerophon at Tlos. Drawing by G. Scharf

Nevertheless, to find Bellerophon represented in the heart of the landscape with which he is traditionally associated is exciting and satisfying. The myths concerning this hero are old ones in Lycia, and some of the most distinguished and ancient Lycian families traced their descent from him.

Away to the east of the track which leads up to the acropolis are substantial remains of Roman buildings, among them a theatre with 34 rows of seats, but the Austrian expedition of 1881 found the ruins so overgrown that they were unable to draw up even the most sketchy plan of the town.

We had no time to explore them, not wishing to risk the adventurous return-journey to Fethiye in darkness. Looking westwards over the Xanthos, crossed now by lengthening shadows, we were almost blinded by the evening sun; but I could just make out the rocky bastion of the acropolis of Pinara in the dark forest of the opposite side of the valley, where the eastern flanks of the massifs of Cragus and Anticragus were already enveloped in a sombre blue.

13

XANTHOS I

The Lycian Acropolis

Xanthos was one of the largest towns of Lycia. Its ruins, which lie some 5 miles north of the estuary of the river Xanthos near the village of Kınık, were discovered by Charles Fellows in 1838. Fellows was so fascinated by the extremely well-preserved relief-covered tombs, the extensive remains of large public buildings and the numerous Lycian inscriptions that he persuaded the British Government to obtain permission from the Sublime Porte to remove the most important antiquities to England. The sculptures which he discovered during three subsequent visits (1839, 1841/2 and 1843/4) were brought back to England by the British Navy and are now in the British Museum.

Marble reliefs from the Harpy-Tomb at Xanthos

Since 1950 Xanthos has been scientifically excavated by French archaeologists whose researches have thrown a great deal of fresh light on the history and architecture of the city and its cemeteries.

Splendidly sited on a hill sloping down southwards and connected by a col to a steep-sided promontory, the city dominated the richest part of the lower Xanthos valley. At the foot of the promontory known as the 'Lycian acropolis' the river forces its way through the last rocky barrage of the valley before reaching the wide coastal plain. As we crossed it on a modern bridge, its turbulent greenish waters swirled round the bottom of the acropolis-rock, Homer's 'eddying Xanthos', by the banks of which Sarpedon, on setting out for Troy, left his wife and baby son and his many possessions.

For Homer, Xanthos is only a river; he never mentions a town of that name. The Lycians themselves seem to have called their city Arñna. It may be that, to begin with, the Xanthians lived in scattered homesteads in the valley and moved to the safety of the hill-top only when altered conditions forced them to defend themselves. In fact, there are no traces of habitation on the acropolis before the 8th century B.C.

The modern track leading up to the ruins runs parallel to the course of the ancient approach-road from the south, above which a Doric triumphal gate erected in honour of the emperor Vespasian (A.D. 69–79) still rears its elegant arch. The main access to the town must always have been from his side where the Lycian acropolis easily commanded the road.

The earliest settlement on this rocky outcrop above the river was destroyed about 540 B.C. when the Persians were besieging it and the Xanthians, according to Herodotus, collected their wives and children in the city and set fire to it before going out themselves to die fighting. This suicidal bravery seems to have impressed the Persians, for during the period of their rule over Asia Minor they interfered little with the internal affairs of the Lycian towns. Herodotus tells us that Xanthos was rebuilt by eighty families who had happened to be absent from the city at the time of the siege.

Some return of prosperity after the disaster is attested on the acropolis itself by the remains of a princely residence with storage-rooms and a temple with three chambers, while on the col to the north of it a necropolis grew up, the most remarkable tomb of which is the so-called Harpy-Tomb, the funerary monument of one of the ruling families.

It belongs to the earliest type of Lycian tomb consisting of a box-like burial chamber, decorated on the outside with reliefs, which rests on a tall, monolithic pillar and is covered with a strongly projecting stone slab stepped back on the underside. The name Harpy-Tomb was applied to it in the 19th century when the mythical creatures—half women, half birds—carved on the reliefs were wrongly thought to be Harpies. They are more probably Sirens, benevolent spirits who carry the souls of the dead, shown here as diminutive female figures, into the beyond. The main scenes of the reliefs (plaster-casts of which have been put up on the monument) represent the dead ancestors as stately figures of enthroned men and women receiving gifts of armour and fertility-symbols such as eggs, cocks, pomegranates and flowers from their descendants, who are carved on a smaller scale. In Lycian belief the dead became heroes, worthy of continual, almost divine veneration, and the tombs were referred to as heroa (singular heroön). But the idea of the soul being

Fighting cocks and hens. Slab of a limestone frieze from a heroön at Xanthos

conveyed into the other world by some friendly spirit is Greek; and Greek sculptors were evidently employed to carve the marble reliefs. Their style reflects Ionian art of the early 5th century B.C.

Just next to the Harpy-Tomb stands a stone sarcophagus of the 4th century B.C. which takes the form of a wooden Lycian house on a tall base. It enclosed reliefs from an earlier pillar-tomb illustrating funerary games, which are now in the museum of Istanbul. When the existing theatre was built in the necropolis during the Roman period, the surviving funerary monuments were left intact as hallowed.

In Byzantine times the upper part of the theatre was incorporated into a defensive wall constructed round the acropolis, in which several statues, fragmentary friezes and relief-decorated pediments of other tombs or shrines were re-used as building material. Fellows demolished this late wall and extracted the sculptures. The French archaeologists who have been working on the acropolis since 1950 have shown that all these sculptures came from three heroa erected on the western side of the acropolis-rock after a violent destruction of the city about 470 B.C., which must be connected with the raids of the

*The Roman theatre of Xanthos with the Harpy-Tomb and the
Sarcophagus-Tomb behind*

Athenian general Cimon along the coast of Asia Minor.

The town quickly recovered from this second catastrophe and entered a period of great prosperity. The reliefs from the three heroa on the acropolis illuminate the artistic influence of both Greece and Persia on Lycian sculpture of that time. Greek in inspiration and style are the pairs of confronted Sphinxes on two of the pediments and so, too, are the scenes on two of the friezes. One shows wild animals pursued by Satyrs armed with sticks, and the other fighting cocks and hens. Traces of colour were still visible on the wings of the Sphinxes and the plumage of the birds when the slabs were freed from the Byzantine wall.

Two other friezes, both of which came from the largest of the three heroa, have themes which go back to oriental prototypes: the funerary repast, inspired by eastern court-ceremonial, and processions of warriors, horsemen and charioteers. Persian influence is particularly striking in the group of a splendid rider-less horse, probably the mount of the deceased, which is being led by a groom, a scene clearly modelled on the horse-leading tribute-bringers carved on the great staircase of the Apadana at Persepolis.

The prolonged Persian rule over Asia Minor has, in fact, left an unmistakable imprint on many Xanthian monuments. A little to the north of the Roman agora or market-square, which extends behind the theatre, stands the 'Inscribed Pillar', one of the most fascinating of the city's tombs, if one of the most ruinous. A slim limestone shaft on a stepped base, its four sides are covered with a long Lycian inscription which has not yet been deciphered, apart fom some proper names which it contains. But on the north side of the monolith there is a Greek epigram of twelve lines which evidently gives the import of the events referred to in the Lycian text. The pillar, which originally carried a burial chamber decorated with reliefs and sculpture in the round, was, as the Greek inscription expressly states, not only a tomb but also a triumphal monument. It is likely that the ruler whom it commemorates was Kherei, the son of Harpagos (only the latter name is preserved), a Lycian dynast known to us from Lycian coins of the later part of the 5th century B.C.

The dead prince vaunts his piety, the splendour of his monument, his physical valour and his military exploits, which included the killing of no less than seven Arcadian hoplites (heavily armed foot-soldiers) in a single day. The tone of oriental despotism is unmistakable here, recalling Assyrian rulers gloating over their holocausts; and something of the same spirit informs the reliefs of the funerary chamber. Some fragments of these were found by Fellows and are in the British Museum, while further pieces have been unearthed by the French excavators and sent to Istanbul. The dynast, shown in Greek armour striding over the prostrate figure of an enemy, is of superhuman size compared with his adversaries. Of these—no doubt the Arcadian foot-soldiers referred to in the inscription—some still appear marching forward in a phalanx holding their shields, others are depicted overcome, stripped and in abject positions of defeat. One warrior still holds his own, but his doom is implied by the triumphal action of the prince who reaches out to touch his shield, a Lycian gesture of triumph. This is the last of the seven shields won by him as trophies; the other six are already shown suspended in a row above.

Eastern influence is also evident in the crowning features of this extra-ordinary tomb. From each corner of the funerary chamber the forepart of a bull carved in the round projected diagonally. The analogy with the bull-capitals of the Achaemenid palaces of Susa and Persepolis is clear. Finally, on top of the stepped horizontal slabs covering the tomb-chamber, a figure of the dynast was seated on a throne formed by the foreparts of two lions; bull and lion traditionally symbolize the power of oriental rulers.

The pride and self-confidence expressed in this monument and the amount of circumstantial detail given in the inscription differ both from the more modest funerary texts of Greece and from the stylized formulae employed in Oriental texts. The tomb of Kherei, as well as his striking coin-portraits, which show him wearing the Persian tiara as symbol of his office, point to an interest in the individual and his unique appearance, for which there is no parallel in the Greek world of that period.

Lycian coin with portrait of Kherei

14

XANTHOS II

The Nereid Monument

ABOUT 400 B.C. some unknown local ruler built the largest and most influential of all Lycian tombs in a spectacular position on a spur of the hill which overlooks the southern approach-road to Xanthos. Destroyed by an earthquake, it was no more than a heap of debris when, in 1838, Fellows first came upon it and discovered two of its sculptured slabs. In the campaign of 1841/2 he excavated the building, which he called 'The Ionic Trophy Monument', and recovered the greater part of four friezes, fragmentary sculptures in the round and a number of architectural fragments which originally formed part of it. But the detailed design of the monument and the disposition of the sculptures on it remained in doubt until the site was thoroughly re-excavated by Professor Demargne and his architect M. Coupel, whose findings have enabled a façade of the building to be reconstructed in the British Museum.

In this monumental tomb the traditional Lycian house-type on a tall podium was replaced by a small Ionic temple of four columns by six. The interior arrangement of the funerary chamber, however, with couches for the dead lining the three sides, repeated the pattern familiar from earlier rock-carved tombs. Despite its hybrid nature, this newly-created architectural model inspired a long series of temple tombs, all of which are significantly situated on the fringe of the Greek world. The most important examples in Asia Minor are the recently discovered heroön at Limyra in eastern Lycia, the Mausoleum of Halicarnassus, the Lion Tomb of Cnidus, the mausoleum at Belevi near Ephesus and the Gümüskesen at Milâs.

The tomb takes its modern name 'Nereid Monument' from the beautiful, life-size figures of girls which were originally disposed between the columns. With almost transparent, billowing chitons pressed against their slender bodies by the wind, they are shown in rapid movement, balanced on fish, birds or turtles, which carry them across the ocean or through the air. The girls are thought to be either Nereids, the Greek mermaids, daughters of the sea-god Nereus, or Aurae, personifications of beneficial breezes. Whatever the name of these spirits of nature, their presence was meant to ensure a safe journey into the beyond for the souls of the dead; their function must, in fact, be the same as that of the Sirens who are represented on the earlier 'Harpy-Tomb'.

Marble figure of a Nereid

The sculptural remains of the tomb also include two groups, each composed of a naked young man carrying off a lightly clad girl; they were originally acroteria or sculptures surmounting each corner of the pediment. Mythological abductions, like that of the daughters of Leucippus by Castor and Polydeuces, or of Oreithyia by Boreas, the North Wind, occur as acroterial decoration on Greek temples, but here on the Nereid Monument the ravishment may have funerary significance and be another allusion to the carrying off of the soul.

Façade of the Nereid Monument in the British Museum

Battle-scene. Slab of a marble frieze from the base of the Nereid Monument

The pedimental reliefs and the friezes have traditional native themes: the glorification of the ruler in war, hunt, feast and sacrifice. But the marble used for the sculptures comes from the Greek islands, and the architect and at least two of the sculptors must have been Greek, though they had Lycian helpers. The monument dates from the end of the 5th century B.C., a period when Greece itself was ravaged as a result of the Peloponnesian War and no longer capable of sustaining grand building-projects. A few of the artists who had previously collaborated in the adornment of the buildings on the Acropolis of Athens may have sought employment in the peripheral regions of Asia Minor, where local dynasties, anxious to perpetuate their fame, were able to commission ambitious artistic schemes.

The reliefs of the Nereid Monument vary greatly in style and quality. The lower and largest of the two friezes surrounding the podium shows sensitively modelled groups of fighting warriors and horsemen—both Persian and Greek—in a noble style which clearly goes back to the Parthenon at Athens.

Heracleia under Latmus. The Temple of Athena and Mount Latmus

A smaller frieze directly above it also portrays battle-scenes, but the spirit here is entirely different. The siege of a city, obviously an historical event, is depicted in lively and original scenes which are, however, based on oriental tradition. A Lycian hill-town with its gates, square and round towers, crenellated walls, houses and monuments is shown with a fascinating attempt at representing spatial depth by foreshortening. Here we can, perhaps, observe a reflection of the experiments in perspective in which Greek painters were engaged at the same period.

The battle is shown in circumstantial detail: we see armies marching in formation; attacking soldiers being repulsed by defenders who, half hidden by the battlements, hurl stones at them; a siege-ladder being raised against the walls for a massed assault; envoys arriving for parley; soldiers carrying off loot; captives being escorted away, and the figure of a woman on the walls of the city who seems, Cassandra-like, to foretell its doom, raising her hands above her head in a dramatic gesture of despair.

The surrender of the defeated town to the victor by a deputation of warriors and elders with sorrowful faces closes the sequence of events. The triumphant

Lycian prince receiving a deputation. Slab of a marble frieze from the base of the Nereid Monument

*Banqueting prince. Slab of a marble frieze from the upper part of the
Nereid Monument*

dynast receives them, seated on a throne with a foot-stool, in the shade of a
parasol held over him by an attendant. The parasol is an old oriental emblem
of divine kingship and although he wears the Persian tiara as a symbol of his
office, this must be a Lycian prince, the ruler who commissioned the monument.

Persian elements are noticeable elsewhere, particularly in the third and
fourth friezes which decorated the entablature and chamber of the monument. The banqueting-scene with the prince as the most important figure
on a couch of his own, attended by hurrying servants and an elderly con-
fidant, goes back to Assyrian court-ceremonial taken over by the Achaemenids.
Propped up on a cushion, the ruler holds a cup and a rhyton, a horn-shaped
vessel ending in the forepart of a winged griffin. This typically Persian
ceremonial vessel was adopted in Greece early in the 5th century B.C. and
eventually became closely associated with the cult of the dead. Persian, too,
is the formal, crimped hair-style and tightly curled beard of the dynast on
the couch. But the most obviously oriental figures occur in the repetitive
processions of tribute-bearers in Greek and Persian dress, and of huntsmen
returning from the chase. Some sections of the third frieze are of poor quality,
with figures of fighting horsemen and foot-soldiers blocked out only roughly
without any attempt to add detail; they look like the work of a local sculptor.

On the east pediment the heroized ruler and his wife are represented enthroned like Zeus and Hera and surrounded by their family and pets, while on the west pediment there is yet another battle of foot-soldiers and cavalry.

Clearly the Lycians were war-like people, and their nobility devoted to the traditional aristocratic pursuits. That a local dynast was able to afford such a showy tomb points to the exceptional wealth of the Xanthos valley. Homer already calls it 'the fat land of Lycia'; and to-day's rich agricultural plains of the lower Xanthos valley still contrast strikingly with the barren mountain regions of central Lycia and with the wooded ranges of Caria.

But more astonishing than the decided ostentation of many Lycian funerary monuments is the almost obsessional concern of this people with the un-violated survival of their tombs. Many of the Greek inscriptions found in Lycia and many of the Lycian inscriptions as far as they can be interpreted, record in minute detail the name of the builder of the tomb and those of the members of his family who alone have the right to be buried in it. Anyone defying these provisions is threatened with the curse of the gods and with heavy fines.

Inscriptions found on several Lycian sites suggest that the chief priest and chief priestess of the Lycians' federal sanctuary kept archives which recorded each new tomb under the day and month of its erection. An organization known as Mindis seems to have been responsible for their preservation and also for collecting the fines imposed on violators of tombs.

15

XANTHOS III

In the first half of the 4th century B.C. a second large necropolis grew up on the south-eastern slopes of the high hill of Xanthos, the so-called 'Roman acropolis'. This area, which is comparatively distant from the 'Lycian acropolis' and from the Nereid Monument, had already once been used as a cemetery in the 6th century B.C. Here, close to an angle in the Hellenistic city-walls, Fellows found the earliest surviving of all Xanthian tombs, the 'Lion Tomb', the only monument which dates from before the Persian destruction of the town. Carved about 560 B.C., the burial chamber was hollowed out of the top of a tall monolithic pillar and decorated in front with a lion killing a bull and a lioness with her young—an old oriental motif. Scenes in low relief on either side celebrate the deeds of the deceased: a hero slaying a lion on one side, and his triumphant return from war on the other. These vigorous, if roughly carved reliefs are now in the British Museum, but the pillar is still to be seen at Xanthos, lying on its side under thickets of ruscus and thorny scrub.

Higher up the slope among sparse trees, the so-called 'Pillar-Tomb' dominates the hillside like a beacon and marks the site of the 4th-century necropolis. This tall limestone shaft, reminiscent of the 'Harpy-Tomb' in its shape, carries a tomb-chamber of undecorated smooth marble slabs, pierced by a small door. It stands on a stepped platform rising above a sheer drop of rock, the face of which is fretted by two tiers of tomb-façades imitating wooden houses with their morticed framework and recessed panels.

Two of the rock-tombs here are of more ambitious design; both were originally preceded by porches composed of separately-carved stone elements. That of the first took the form of the open wooden porch of a native Lycian house, while the other, which lies a little further to the west, was treated as the front of an Ionic temple, no doubt an echo of the Nereid Monument. The door of the second tomb, which is framed by delicate Greek mouldings, was closed by a sliding stone panel. Inside the square chamber are rock-cut funerary couches fashioned as wooden beds with carved legs.

Just below the rocky shelf on which the 'Pillar Tomb' stands and a little to the east of it, Fellows found a richly carved sarcophagus on a high base which, according to its inscriptions, was built by the Lycian official Payava. Only the lower part of the tomb on a base of three steps now remains in

Two Lycian warriors on the south side of the Tomb of Payava in the British Museum

position. All the relief-covered superstructure was removed to the British Museum by Fellows. But during clearing-operations carried out round the base in 1952 by the French mission, a missing corner of the sarcophagus with the first figure from its west side—a Persian officer in trousers and a belted tunic—and the corresponding figure from the north side—a youth in a short tunic—was discovered; it is now in the museum of Antalya. The scenes carved on the box of the sarcophagus and on its ogival roof are of exceptional interest.

On the west side of the box appears a bearded Persian satrap, probably Autophradates, who ruled in Sardis between 390 and 350 B.C. and whose name seems to be mentioned in a Lycian inscription above. Seated on a draped throne to give audience, he wears typical Persian clothes: a soft tiara on his head, a sleeved coat thrown over his shoulders, a tunic with wrist-length sleeves, long trousers, and a sheathed Median dagger hanging from his belt.

The elaborate dress of the satrap and his attendants reflects an oriental convention, according to which human dignity and rank are always expressed through formal attire. In striking contrast with this, the Greeks always conveyed mental and physical excellence through the perfection of the naked human body; and the Lycian nobles who appear standing before the satrap and on the short sides of the sarcophagus are represented according to Greek ethos. Although clad in scanty Greek dress and in Greek armour modelled on the naked male torso, they are, nevertheless, characterized as Lycians by their shoulder-length hair—a fashion unknown in contemporary Greece.

One of the bearded, long-haired warriors on the south side may be Payava (whose name is mentioned on this side as well as on the east side of the tomb); and the naked athlete crowned by an elderly man on the north side perhaps represents the youthful Payava as a victor in an athletic contest, a motif which appears on other Lycian funerary monuments and seems to be inspired by Greek prototypes.

The armed horseman riding down a foot-soldier in the midst of a pitched battle in mountainous landscape on the east side is almost certain to be Payava. Beside the usual Greek cavalry equipment he wears a stiff leather apron attached to his waist at the back and to the horse's collar in front to protect the rider's legs and the animal's flanks, the 'parameridia' which Xenophon, the ancient historian and writer on horsemanship, mentions as being used by Persian riders. The same piece of equipment appears again on the relief with a battle-scene carved on one side of the ridge of the sarcophagus' roof, the other side of which is decorated with huntsmen pursuing a gazelle, a boar and a bear.

It has plausibly been suggested that the audience-scene on the box of the sarcophagus is connected with the Lycians' involvement in the great rising of the satraps against the Persian king between 367 and 360 B.C. Like the earlier tomb of Kherei, that of Payava is a fascinating illustration of Lycia's penetration by both Persian and Greek elements.

While the scenes on the sarcophagus itself are obviously representations of actual historical events, the decoration of the roof has a symbolic character. On both sides of the curved ridge-roof, just above the lifting-bosses in the form of foreparts of lions, appears a four-horse chariot speeding along with a fully armed warrior beside the charioteer. Although chariot races in which warriors jumped on and off at full speed formed part of the military training of the nobleman, these scenes must be understood as relating to the funerary aspect of such races and probably refers to the heroization of the dead. The seated figures in the gable-ends are perhaps ancestors of Payava, and the sphinxes above them symbolize the beyond.

Another large sarcophagus of the 4th century B.C. was found by Fellows on the lower eastern slopes of the 'Roman acropolis 'outside the Hellenistic city-walls. According to the inscription on the rectangular box of the tomb, it belonged to the officer Merehi. Only the ogival roof, which had already

The roof of the sarcophagus of Merehi in the British Museum

The sarcophagus of Merehi at Xanthos

been thrown down by an earthquake, was brought back to London by Fellows. It is adorned on the crest with a frieze of battle-scenes, incidents of daily life including the crowning of a victorious athlete, and with a banquet. Large-scale reliefs on the curving slopes of the roof again show the four-horse chariots with fully armed warriors beside the charioteer. Under the hooves of the team on one side appears a figure of the Chimaera, the famous Lycian monster. As the armed nobleman in the chariot above is not Bellerophon, we may assume that the Chimaera has been carved here as a heraldic symbol showing that the line of Merehi traced its descent from Bellerophon.

The sarcophagus itself is a large rectangular stone box simulating a wooden construction; and with one end tilting up from the surrounding wilderness of rock and low scrub it resembles a wooden ark tossed by the sea—an unquiet grave indeed. Above it the lowering eastern bluff of the acropolis is pierced by a row of fifteen rock-tombs of the 4th century B.C. The area outside the city to the north-east has not yet been fully explored; it must have been the main necropolis of Xanthos in later centuries.

Within the circuit of the Hellenistic walls in the eastern sector of the town is situated an isolated sarcophagus of the late 4th century B.C., known as 'Sarcophagus of the Dancing Girls'. Its ogival roof, which now lies on the ground split in two, is carved on its short sides with pairs of dancing girls in short swirling tunics facing each other. These elegant creatures, pirouetting on tiptoe, their richly curled hair flying out behind them, are based on Greek prototypes of the later 5th century B.C., perhaps the figures of 'Laconian dancers' created, according to Pliny, by the sculptor Callimachus. Here the motif has been adapted for funerary use; ritual dances seem to have formed part of Lycian burial ceremonial.

On the curved slopes of the sarcophagus' roof above the massive lifting-bosses more traditional Lycian scenes are represented: a boar-hunt on one side and the outcome of a battle on the other. On the left the victor stands on a rocky pinnacle and touches the suspended shield of his vanquished enemy in the Lycian gesture of triumph, while below him the terrified horse of his opponent gallops away to the right, the stripped rider slipping helplessly from its back.

The extensive area between the eastern city-wall, the Lycian acropolis and the Roman acropolis (on top of which the remains of a large Byzantine monastery and of a temple have been identified) has not yet been explored. This sloping ground was obviously terraced in antiquity, but is now overgrown by broom and low, thorny scrub, under which the ruins are largely hidden. Here lay the residential and commercial quarters of the city which must have reached a considerable size in the Roman and Byzantine period.

The only building being excavated by the French mission at present is an Early Christian church in the eastern part of the town. We were shown its apse with stepped semicircular seating for the bishop and clergy and, in the north aisle, a beautiful floor-mosaic of deer flanking a vase from which flows the water of life. Destroyed (presumably by Arab sea-raiders in the 7th century A.D.) and later re-used in the Middle Byzantine period, the basilica retains vestiges of frescoes of the 10th–11th century A.D. at the east end of the nave. Among faded saintly companions the elongated figure of St Stephen holding his censer is comparatively well preserved.

The city's decline which began with the Arab raids was probably aggravated by the silting-up of the river-mouth, and by the 12th century A.D. Xanthos had sunk into oblivion.

Dancing girls. Relief on the roof of a Lycian sarcophagus at Xanthos

16

PATARA

AFTER lunching with our French friends at the Letoön, we crossed the Xanthos again and headed due south. In that direction a range of low hills bars the view of the sea, and hidden behind them lie the ruins of Patara, once one of the principal harbours of Lycia.

Through these coastal hills, scoured by the sea-winds, we followed a narrow gorge to a sheltered triangular plain. Off to the right among fruit trees and small patches of fields lies a deserted village. The insalubrious plains are usually abandoned during the hot months for the cooler uplands of the interior, where the villagers camp in the 'yaila' with all their livestock and essential household implements.

Along the foot of a wooded ridge our track skirted a widening reedy creek, the upper reaches of the ancient harbour which has been silted up since the Middle Ages. Remains of sarcophagi and stone-built tombs of the Roman period, some of them with well-preserved coffered vaults, emerged from thickets of bay and myrtle lining the wayside. Where the plain suddenly opens out towards the sea stands a triple arch, the city's main gateway, its crisp limestone façade radiant in the afternoon light. The three arches are flanked by consoles which once supported portrait busts of the family of Mettius Modestus, a Roman governor of Lycia. Over each arch is a blank niche and the monument is crowned by a Doric frieze and a cornice bearing a Greek inscription which proclaims Patara the metropolis of the Lycian people.

In a field beyond the arch a group of typically Lycian sarcophagi with ogival roofs serves as a reminder that, however Romanized in its main surviving monuments, Patara was a Lycian town, the home of that essentially Lycian god, Apollo. Of the famous temple of Apollo Patroös no trace has been found to date. Captain Beaufort, who surveyed this coast in 1811, fancifully identified as the oracle of Apollo a sunken circular building with a central pillar, which he found on the hill above the theatre; but it is, in fact, no more than a large rock-cut cistern. Curiously, the god's oracle at Patara is said to have operated only during the six winter months. In the summer, so it was believed, Apollo spent his time on the island of Delos—the place of his birth—presumably on a well-earned holiday.

After driving as far as we could over scorched stubble, we left our car in

The Roman arch at Patara

the shade of a clump of holm-oaks in the neighbourhood of the theatre.
Immense sand-dunes pressing against its south-west flank and engulfing the
orchestra and part of the auditorium strikingly illustrate the fate of Patara
as a whole: alluvial sand carried by the prevailing south wind ultimately
extinguished the life of the entire city, which depended for its livelihood
on a functioning port. The auditorium is carved from the northern slope
of a rocky outcrop which rises abruptly from the plain near the shore. The
masonry of the stage-building of pale biscuit colour is beautifully preserved
on the east side. On the wall by the right parodos or lateral entrance to the

orchestra, the dedicatory inscription of Quintus Velius Titianus and of his daughter Velia Procla survives; it dates from the middle of the 2nd century A.D.

The emperor Hadrian, an obsessive traveller, visited Patara in A.D. 130 with his wife Sabina, and inscriptions record that statues were set up to them in honour of that occasion. Saint Paul, a more austere but no less indefatigable traveller, had changed ship at Patara at an earlier date.

A vast, fen-like depression to the west of the town marks the extent of the old harbour. Something of its commercial importance can be glimpsed in the ruins of a large granary on its western edge. Like a similar building in Andriake, an ancient port further east near the city of Myra, it had a two-storeyed façade decorated above the doors with pairs of brackets for busts. Behind the façade are eight long, barrel-vaulted rooms set side by side, each with its door and a window above. Sir William Gell, who visited Patara in the early 19th century, saw an inscription on the granary stating that it was built in the reign of the emperor Trajan (A.D. 98–117).

To the north of the theatre, much overgrown and not easy to approach through dunes of loose sand and swampy stretches, lies a Corinthian temple, the walls and richly carved entrance of which are well preserved to a considerable height. Further to the south-east are the Baths of Vespasian (A.D. 69–79), while another Roman bathing establishment is situated in the neighbourhood of the Triple Gate.

The size of Patara and the excellent preservation of many of its buildings would make scientific excavation a rewarding task.

17

KAŞ—ANTIPHELLOS

OUR road eastwards skirted at first the north flank of the hills which cut Patara off from the lower Xanthos valley. The low-lying fields to the left, hemmed in between this coastal range and the southern spurs of the Dumanlı Dağ, used to be a vast marsh, productive only of leeches which were exported in large quantities for medicinal purposes in the 19th century. Now drainage has enabled cotton to be grown here, and groups of white-scarfed women were gathering the crop.

A bumpy causeway crossing the depression took us to the foot of the coastal cliffs which form the southern fastnesses of the Lycian mountains. Here a road has been blasted along the rock-face half-way between the crest of the precipice and the sea. Fresh reddish-white scars showed the recent activity of bulldozers. The surface was a coarse, shifting gravel of razor sharpness with frequent eruptions of underlying bed-rock.

We climbed higher and higher in a succession of vertiginous curves. Although most of our attention was focused on keeping a respectful distance from the precipitous edge and on avoiding outcropping lumps of rock, we were able to cast an occasional glance at the ever expanding view to the south. The late afternoon sun gilded the barren crags and headlands jutting into the deepest Prussian-blue sea, and each rocky promontory was outlined by a shimmering necklet of breaking waves. Tufts of spiny spurge and low cushions of cistus were clinging to the inhospitable slopes above us, where I twice caught a tantalizing glimpse of stretches of ancient masonry. But this was no time for archaeology: the shades were lengthening and we had been warned against driving here by night. One side of the sheltered bay of Kalkan, which suddenly opened below us on the right, was already plunged into dusky blue. A small white mosque and neat houses ringing the miniature port looked temptingly secure and homely, but we decided to press on to Kaş, the ancient Antiphellos.

In the south the small islands of Çatal Ada and Rho resembled ships anchored out at sea. Further east, on the horizon, the deepening evening shadows threw into relief the indented bays and folded hills of the island of Castellorizo and the long, low promontory of Kaş curving out towards it from the mainland.

We reached the fjord-like western bay of Antiphellos just as its wooded slopes were illuminated by the setting sun. Like the more open bay of Sevedo on the other side of the headland, it must have served as a harbour in antiquity. To-day is it deserted. Some ancient walls still straggle down through the macchia from the crest of the ridge to the water's edge. The landscape here seemed softer than the wild crags we had hugged during our drive. The outlines of the hills by the shore are gentle and clad in luxuriant vegetation, as the sheltering foreland tames the fierceness of the open sea; and in the low bluffs on the landward side appear the quiet unchanging façades of rock-cut Lycian tombs overhung by trees.

In the fast-fading light we lurched down a bumpy lane into the modern village of Kaş. Turning right by a small mosque into the road which leads to the Greek theatre, we passed the handsome ruin of a large ancient building on the left. Just beyond this ruin is the modest concrete box of the Günay Motel, where we managed to secure a cell-like room for the night. It opened on to a narrow communal terrace overlooking the sea.

Too exhausted to think of setting out for a meal immediately, we remained seated on the terrace for a while. In the evening light the view spread out before us had, for all its grandeur, a soothing effect. Below the Motel huge rocks and loose boulders fall away steeply into the sea. The great depth of water here must have made this stretch of the coast quite unsuitable for anchorage. A little further east, a shallower bay, protected by a cluster of rocks—probably the remains of an ancient pier—sheltered a few small craft. The hills beyond it held an afterglow of the sunset, as if illuminated from within.

Across the pale evening sea came the twinkling harbour lights of Castellorizo, a Greek island. Its Turkish name Meïs must be a corruption of the classical Megiste (the largest island). Until the Turkish War of Independence Kaş was inhabited largely by Greeks from Castellorizo. Though barren and unproductive itself, Castellorizo served as a provisioning-post for all the early travellers to Lycia. Sea-born trade made it a flourishing commercial centre, and there was constant traffic between the island and the scala of Andifilo, as Kaş was then called. Now there is no commerce between the two. War and politics have disrupted what was a natural and easy symbiosis. Kaş is visited regularly by a Turkish coastal steamer, but it is too cut off from its hinterland to serve as a port for southern Lycia.

In the mild dusk we walked down to the centre of the village, a semicircle of white-washed houses—some with prettily carved balconies and lattices—facing the calm harbour-basin. Further along the curved quayside two teashops, hospitably lit by oil-lamps, hummed with the men's quiet talk and the clicking of trick-track. We chose the lokanta right at the end of the harbour, a couple of barrel-vaulted rooms with their arched ends opening towards the quay. The promising odour of a charcoal grill emerged from here, and we sat down by the water's edge and ordered fish. We waited its preparation contentedly, listening to the clucking and gurgling of the sea in the harbour-wall and sipping red wine. By our feet a small army of cats waited with corresponding patience.

Slowly the neighbouring tables filled with customers, all of them male; there was not a single female face to relieve the monotony. Occasionally one of the small boys playing by the quayside ran up to his father and snatched a bite. As darkness fell, the local womenfolk, their hair decently covered by scarfs, assembled with their needlework in a segregated group under a street light. Presumably they had all already eaten in the privacy of their homes. Shuttling erratically between mothers and fathers, the children gave the impression of holding together the fabric of family life. But most of their games centred on a couple of battered Corinthian capitals turned upside down and a piece of richly carved entablature with an inscription, referring—so far as we could make out in the uncertain light and between dangling legs—to the people of Antiphellos and Patara.

If we disregard electric power and the occasional steamer, life for the inhabitants of modern Kaş probably goes on in much the same way as it did for the ancient Antiphellians. Camels and donkeys are still a more reliable form of transport in these parts than the over-worked and under-serviced lorries. But things are changing fast. Once the coast-road is asphalted, the volume of motor-traffic will grow and with it the inevitable concrete boxes of tourist hotels and souvenir-shops, neon-lighting and night-clubs . . . a dismal prospect.

We were up early next morning after a restless night, but a breakfast of flat, pancake-like bread, rose petal jam and tea, served on the terrace in the rising sun, compensated us for our nocturnal discomforts.

After breakfast we set out to look at the Greek theatre of Antiphellos. A little way beyond the Motel to the west, the path comes to an end and we climbed over a wooden fence into a sparse olive grove. Here, isolated on a barren slope, stands the small Hellenistic theatre overlooking the sea. The absence of a stage-building makes for a striking purity of line. The auditorium, which is preserved almost to its full height, rests against the hillside without vaulted substructures and the grey-limestone seats are undercut to give more room. Two radial staircases divide the auditorium into three wedges and there is another flight of stairs at each side. From the topmost row of seats the eye travels unhindered, beyond Castellorizo, to the southern horizon where sea and sky merge.

Further up the hill and east of the theatre lies one of the extensive ancient cemeteries of Antiphellos. Its most remarkable tomb is carved largely from a cubic outcrop of rock and takes the form of a Greek house with pilasters at the corners and a Doric frieze. The interior contained the usual funerary couches, but the niche opposite the door is decorated with a relief frieze of twenty-five tiny figures of women who join hands in a ritual dance, which makes the stylized folds of their dresses fly out in a decorative pattern. This unique tomb probably dates from the 4th century B.C.

To the same period belongs a splendid sarcophagus tomb of the traditional type imitating wooden construction, which stands on a tall base in the village to the north-east of the harbour. The lifting-bosses on the ogival roof are carved in the form of lions' foreparts and the base bears a Lycian inscription.

Xanthos. The Pillar Tomb

18

DEMRE—MYRA

FROM Kaş we wound uphill in great curves, at first through orange and lemon groves, then through olive plantations and finally through the bare crags of the coastal range again. Before turning inland, we stopped for a moment to enjoy the landscape spread map-like below: from this height the configuration of the headland of Kaş resembles a dolphin plunging south-westwards into the shimmering sea.

A totally different world awaited us inland. As soon as the sea had dis-appeared from sight, the barren, carst-like ground seemed to drain this scenery of all memory of water. To the north and west the hostile-looking shoulders of Massicytus, bleached to the colour of a skeleton by the fierce light, and the barrier of the appropriately named Susuz Dağ (Waterless Mountain) tower over the lesser ranges of the middle distance. We crossed a succession of dry little plains. Divided by low ridges, they have retained in their centres fertile reserves of reddish soil, eroded and washed down from the surrounding hills. Here some profitable form of agriculture has always been carried on. Between rocky outcrops parched stubble-fields show that in spring corn has grown here in earth saturated by winter snow and rain.

The roughly triangular plateau of Demre is itself absolutely devoid of rivers, though the Demre Çay, the ancient river Myrus, has carved a precipi-tous gorge along its north and east sides. Despite the harshness of its nature and its limited accessibility this limestone plateau nourished a surprisingly large number of small Lycian towns in antiquity. They may have prized their remoteness and resulting independence. Their cisterns, their fields and their flocks seem to have supported a style of life comfortable enough to allow their rulers to build spectacular funerary monuments for themselves and their families, while lesser mortals were able to afford at least an undecorated sarcophagus. Such plain sarcophagi of Lycian type stand out along our route from time to time among low scrub and clusters of Vallonia oak, forbidding grey hulks, their surface pitted by weathering.

Occasionally we saw Yürük tents in the distance: long ridges of dark goat's hair cloth propped up on poles, with children and animals around them. There are a few villages, but their dun-coloured mud walls, criss-crossed by bleached and crooked timbers, barely stand out from the almost identical shades and patterns of the surrounding landscape.

Near the centre of the plateau the slightly larger village of Yavu is situated under a towering wall of smooth rock. The greyish-blue colour of this perpendicular limestone cliff may have given the name Kyaneai—the blue ones —to the ancient city which lies, out of sight, on its northern summit. High up in the rock face a number of tombs are carved, some with Greek temple-façades, others of simpler Lycian type. They are all on a modest scale compared with what we had met in the more fertile regions of western Lycia. What distinguishes them is their soaring height and seeming inaccessibility.

As we were leaving Yavu, two boys who had watched us from a slight rise, where they were minding a flock of goats, threw stones at our car; the inhospitable landscape seemed to have left its mark on its inhabitants. Climbing over the low ridge which divided us from the next plain, we noticed a bank of sinister-looking clouds in the distance, which seemed to rise from the rocky ground. The phenomenon appeared inexplicable until we realized that we were approaching the Demre Gorge and that the vapours emerged, not from the dry limestone plateau itself, but from the deep chasm bordering it on the north-east. From its depth the humidity of the Demre Çay drifts up in the form of clouds; and in that quarter the whole sky was becoming hazy and the air oppressive.

To the north, on heights overlooking the Demre Gorge, lies the site of Gjölbashi, the ancient city of Trysa, which was discovered by the German scholar J. A. Schönborn in 1841. The most important surviving building there is the heroön or monumental tomb of a local ruler. Next to the gate of the sacred precinct surrounding the tomb is a relief of Bellerophon charging on his winged horse Pegasus against the Chimaera, a subject from which we can infer that the owner of the tomb, like other Lycian nobles at Tlos and Xanthos, derived his descent from this mythical hero. The whole inner face of the precinct-wall and, on the entrance side, the outer face, too, were decorated with super-imposed friezes in low relief. The familiar themes of Lycian sepulchral art, such as banquets and dances, are interspersed with scenes from Greek mythology and episodes from the *Iliad* and *Odyssey*. This choice of subjects shows how deep an influence Greek culture had on the rulers of even so remote a mountain city as Trysa in the early 4th century B.C.

After Schönborn's discovery of the tomb its existence was all but forgotten until 1881, when a team of Austrian archaeologists excavated it and removed the sculptured slabs to Vienna, where they are now in the Kunsthistorisches Museum. Apart from the heroön and a few lesser tombs beside the enclosure, the ancient town of Trysa still awaits scientific excavation.

As we reached the eastern tip of the plateau, the view ahead and to the south opened out. In the middle distance the ruins of what appeared to be a Hellenistic fortress were visible among encroaching scrub. Beyond it, through the hazy midday glare, we made out the next great mountain-range

Temple-tomb near Myra

stretching southwards into the sea: the Alaja Dağ with the promontory of Cape Fineka. Hemmed in between it and the Demre plateau lies the alluvial plain of the Demre Çay. From our elevated position we could see no more than its eastern end, filled by an extensive lagoon of glaucous blue and divided from the sea by a spit of reddish sand.

Our road turned south and then sharply west, beginning the long descent into the coastal plain, much of it green and well cultivated with groves of olives and citrus fruit spreading around the outlying villages of Demre. In-

Rock-cut funerary reliefs at Myra

visible to us beyond a coastal ridge in the west is the land-locked harbour of Andriake, while a little further inland, over a saddle of low hills, lies the ancient city of Sura.

At the foot of these hills, where our road finally turned away from the scarred face of the plateau, we noticed a large temple-tomb. Although of Roman date, it still retains the Lycian arrangement of a plain podium containing the lower tomb chamber and surmounted by the tomb proper in the form of a temple. The fine ashlar masonry of the cella with its Corinthian corner pilasters and blank pediments has weathered to a warm shade of russet.

Over the doorway is a richly carved lintel in a good state of preservation. Three sides of the oblong interior are fitted with stone benches for sarcophagi, which were framed by shallow arches.

The village of Demre, the ancient Myra, was deserted in the midday heat. More by instinct than by knowledge, we found our way to the church of Saint Nicholas, identifiable by a cluster of dark cypresses towering above the guardian's hut by the roadside. From here a broad ramp leads down into a pit in which a group of buildings has been marooned by the ever rising level of the alluvial deposits of the Demre Çay. An improvised roof of red tiles shelters a ruined Byzantine church, of which the triple apse although covered in weeds is comparatively well preserved. The dark interior retains a polychrome marble floor, vestiges of frescoes flaking from the dank walls and some nameless tombs: a gloomy and depressing place compared with the abodes the Lycians carved for their dead, high above the ground, lifted into the brightness of the sky.

The parsimoniously restored basilica next door is equally unprepossessing. In a corner of the south aisle a damaged marble sarcophagus, said to be that from which the bones of Saint Nicholas were looted by merchants of Bari in 1087, reveals the poverty of the early church. A Roman work of about A.D. 170–180, it was originally carved with figured arcades, now badly mutilated. On its lid, which is in the form of a couch, a couple recline, their battered features staring vacantly into space. If this is indeed the tomb of the saintly bishop, there is perhaps divine retribution in the fact that Saint Nicholas' bones suffered the same fate as those of the original occupant of the sarcophagus. But no doubt the saint's relics fared better in the end, being rehoused in a splendid shrine in the huge Romanesque basilica built in his honour at Bari in Southern Italy. And his fame, which had always been great in Mediterranean lands, spread north and west. As the patron saint of ships and sailors, he is the direct descendant of the powerful pagan protectors of seafarers—Poseidon and the Dioscuri—and is still held in high regard by the orthodox Greeks. He is also, of course, the childrens' saint, whence Santa Claus, our Father Christmas, and a sad degeneration into commercialism.

From Saint Nicholas we made our way through orchards to the foot of the Demre plateau, on the easternmost summit of which the walls of the acropolis of ancient Myra are just visible. The south-west and east faces of the limestone cliffs beneath the acropolis are honeycombed with the most varied and closely-packed Lycian tombs to be found anywhere. By a curious effect of weathering the carved tomb-façades glow in a reddish-brown tone which makes them stand out at a distance from the cool greyish-blue of the unworked rock.

In the security of Roman imperial rule the town of Myra spread from its confined eagle's nest into the open valley below where the Demre Çay (the ancient river Myrus) emerges from its gorge. Secular buildings grew up in the

Rock-tombs at Myra

area originally reserved for the necropolis. We passed the remains of a Roman bathing establishment and, leaving the car by the dry bed of a torrent, proceeded on foot to the main part of the western necropolis. Carved one above another in every suitable perpendicular surface or free-standing outcrop of rock, the Lycian tombs here seem a textbook illustration of all the possible variations on the theme of wooden architectural form translated into stone. Every conceivable variation from the simplest undecorated house-doorway to the most elaborately carved and painted temple façade appears to be represented; but the majority of the tombs show the Lycian house-front: a porch with a flat roof of an ogival or triangular pediment. Many of the tombs are carved with figures in high relief, sometimes beside the entrance, sometimes on the pillars of the porch and sometimes inside it. The figures are often

Rock-tombs at Myra. Drawing by G. Scharf

of life size and can be made out with ease from below. The themes of these reliefs include the traditional scenes of youths arming, battles and funerary banquets. There are also scenes of family life, intimate and touching in domestic detail. Charles Fellows and the French traveller, Texier, both of whom saw the reliefs in the 1830s, found extensive remains of colour preserved on them; and even now traces of polychromy survive on some of the tombs in the eastern necropolis.

The immense *cavea* of the Roman theatre leans against the tomb-riddled flank of the mountain. Supported by two concentric semicircles of tall vaulted substructions, the rows of seats still rise to a considerable height. The orchestra has been cleared of earth and scrub, and many fragments of the tall stage building which had an elaborate columnar façade, now largely collapsed, are neatly piled in front of it.

19

FINIKE AND LIMYRA

AFTER crossing the turbid waters of the Demre Çay, which has washed up mounds of shingle on its eastern bank, the road east soon becomes rugged again. It is confined between the lower reaches of the Alaja Dağ and the lagoon. Earlier travellers have described the mountain crossing from Myra to Finike as among the worst to be met with. But the modern road keeps to sea level; blasted along the limestone crags, it gashes the rock face of the coast with a raw reddish streak. At the far end of the lagoon, where the sea laps over a smooth ridge of sand, the bleached framework of a fishing establishment stands like a skeleton.

Rounding a small promontory, we left all trace of human life behind to drive for the next two hours through a pitiless waste of glaring rock and glistening sea. In vain we looked for the shade of a bush to picnic in. This was an inanimate world of crystalline shapes and surfaces whose sole purpose seemed to be to reflect and intensify the heat of the sun. Suddenly the hypnotic monotony of the scorched road ahead was relieved by a living creature. Something small and elongated moved awkwardly over the coarse gravel. Denys pulled up to investigate: it was a chameleon. Although lumbering over pinkish ground, it remained obstinately bright green until it disappeared in a fissure of the rock. There followed another succession of barren coves and promontories of lunar bleakness. After a final twist round a steep bluff, the fertile plain of Finike opened out before us, its unbroken green arc, rimmed by a band of gleaming sand, sweeping round to the south. Bordered in the west and north by a semicircle of mountains, its easternmost point abuts against the Chelidonian headland, where the wild tangle of rocky ridges falls away into the sea. Along the edge of this fertile crescent a number of ancient Lycian towns were situated: Gagae, Corydalla, Limyra and Phoenicus, the present Finike. Between the eastern flank of the Alaja Dağ and the bed of the Bashgöz Çay, the Arycandus of antiquity, lies the small modern town with an asphalted main street, a couple of hotels and lokantas and a modest lido consisting of a row of concrete huts which can be hired by enterprising holiday-makers.

Our goal was Limyra, which lies slightly north-east of Finike, at the foot of a steep mountain and close to the sources of the river Limyrus. During the first half of the 4th century B.C. the Lycian town of Limyra seems to have been ruled by a king whose name, Perikle, is mentioned on inscriptions and on coins bearing his portrait. The only facts known about him from ancient writers are that he besieged Phaselis, a town on the east coast of the Chelidonian headland, and captured Telmessus (Fethiye) in western Lycia. He must have taken the Greek name Pericles in admiration of the great Athenian statesman of the 5th century B.C. This esteem of Greek culture and personalities which characterizes so many of the Lycian dynasts of the 5th and 4th centuries B.C. did not prevent them from entertaining excellent relations with the Persian satraps. Under their local rulers the Lycian cities managed their affairs relatively unhampered by foreign interference. Although they

Lycian coin with portrait of King Perikle

had to pay tribute and were required to supply troops and ships to the Great King, they retained their national identity and a virtual independence.

But Perikle was to be the last of the autonomous feudal rulers. Under him the Lycians joined the ill-fated satraps' revolt, after the collapse of which their territory was handed over to Mausolus who, though implicated at an early stage in the plot, had wisely changed his allegiance and retained the favour of the Persian king. On Mausolus' untimely death in 353 B.C., other members of his family succeeded him and the house of the Hekatomnids ruled Lycia until the conquest of Alexander the Great.

With the disappearance of the native princes, the Lycian cities became republics, but they kept their old federal traditions and developed what were probably the most successful democratic institutions of the ancient world. By the end of the 4th century their Hellenization was almost complete. The native language and script, which had survived side by side with the Greek so far, now disappears, and the Lycians' national identity slowly merges in the supranational civilization created by Alexander the Great, whose genius gave a cultural unity to Greece and the Near Eastern world for centuries to come.

The first traveller to visit the site of Limyra seems to have been C. R. Cockerell in 1811, whose copy of a bilingual inscription in Greek and Lycian carved on a sarcophagus tomb in the western necropolis there stimulated the earliest researches into the Lycian language. Fellows followed in 1838 and collected a large number of further inscriptions in the necropolis, while shortly afterwards Spratt and Forbes identified the acropolis of the ancient city on top of a steep conical hill projecting from the mountain-range just north of the theatre.

On this rocky crag recent excavation by German archaeologists has revealed not only extensive fortifications dating from the Persian period, but also an artificial terrace cut into the southern extremity of the hill-top, on which once stood the richly-carved heroön of a local ruler. A fair number of sculptured fragments of the building survive, and their unusual character was clearly inspired by Athenian architectural prototypes. The few Greek letters of a dedicatory inscription preserved on the podium of the temple-like structure can be dated to the 4th century B.C., but they unfortunately do not mention the name of the occupant. However, it seems highly unlikely that such a splendid funerary monument based on Athenian models would have belonged to anybody other than King Perikle himself, and the excavation which Dr Borchhardt and his colleagues have been carrying out since 1969 has done much to confirm this attractive theory.

Following the Elmalı road from Finike as far as Turuncova, we turned right on to a track which skirts the foot of the mountain to the village of Yuvalılar. This straggling place which has grown up on the site of Limyra seems to be of fairly recent origin. There are wooden houses among gardens of fruit trees and olives and a few low concrete buildings, but the almost barren slopes of the steep hill to the left are dotted with large numbers of black tents pitched within rough enclosures of brushwood. A good proportion of the inhabitants must still be semi-nomadic.

Opposite the school-house at the end of a grassy track bordered by a runnel of water lies a farm-house which the German archaeologists have rented as a dig-house. We found only the Turkish excavation commissioner there, comfortably clad in striped pyjamas, who told us that his German colleagues were all up on the mountain. We turned to look at the precipitous height behind us, near the summit of which the minute white cone of a tent stood out from the naked rock. Our hearts sank. The thought of climbing up there in the afternoon heat was daunting. The ascent takes about 35 minutes, and twice a day a boy with a donkey carrying water makes the trip to provide for the architects, the restorer and the Kurdish workmen who camp up there. As this boy was just about to set out, I gave him a note for Dr Borchhardt informing him of our arrival.

Meanwhile we decided to look at the antiquities of the lower town and to leave the visit to the heroön for early next morning. The slopes of the hillside flanking the acropolis are striated with curiously regular curved ribs of limestone running from the north-east down to the south-west. Into the upright face of these strata of rock innumerable tomb-façades are cut next to each other in ever descending lines. These again are of various types, some imitating wooden house-fronts, others temple-façades with Ionic columns, pediments and acroteria. The finer details of the façades were often rendered in paint. Beside some of the tombs quiet family scenes are carved in a delicate low relief: a husband in a light, billowing garment facing his veiled wife and baby son across the door of the tomb; or a man and his three boys advancing from the left towards the porch, greeted by a woman and her young daughter on the right. Other reliefs represent funerary banquets, and there are a few spirited battle-scenes.

Walking east towards the theatre, we passed a well-preserved stretch of the Roman fortifications of the town: nine projecting towers linked by curtain-walls, the whole constructed of brick, stone and mortar and incorporating much earlier material. South of the walls, in luscious green gardens, rises the river Limyrus and meanders across the plain towards the sea at Finike.

The Roman theatre is on the left of the road, resting against the barren hillside. Its overgrown cavea has been robbed of almost all its stone seating, and of the stage building only the lowest part remains. Carved fragments of the entablature of the architecturally treated stage front peep from behind a wilderness of weeds.

On the declivity to the east of the theatre a further necropolis is situated. Of particular interest is a sarcophagus of Lycian type on a tall base and surmounted by an ogival roof. According to its Lycian inscription, it belonged to a nobleman by the name of Chñtabura, who may have been a relation of King Perikle. The reliefs carved on the lower part of the monument were first made known by Fellows, but a recent study by Dr Borchhardt has thrown fresh light on them.

In addition to the traditional motifs of a funerary repast and sacrifice on the south side of the base and a four-horse chariot with a fully armed warrior on the north, a more esoteric scene appears on the west. The naked youth discarding his garment on this side seems to represent the dead man divesting himself of all his earthly honours and attributes before approaching the judges of the underworld, two of whom, long-haired and bearded elders, are

Relief on the west side of the sarcophagus of Chñtabura at Limyra

seated on either side of him. According to the myth recorded in Plato's *Gorgias* and also in the *Apology*, of the three judges of the dead the one who is responsible for deciding the fate of the people of Asia is Rhadamantys. Here we should probably recognize Rhadamantys in the old man on the right who detains the dead with a gentle gesture of his raised hand, as he delivers judgement.

The figure on the left would then be another judge, either Aiakos or Minos. This adaptation of Platonic ideas is a further proof of the deep penetration of Greek thought into Lycia at this period. It may perhaps be significant that the judgement-scene is carved on the west side of the tomb, traditionally the direction in which the land of the dead was thought to lie.

When we returned to the dig-house, we were shown the latest finds from excavations at the foot of the sarcophagus of Chñtabura: a Lycian coin, fragmentary stone wings belonging, perhaps, to figures of sphinxes, and the leg of a horse. These free-standing figures may have decorated the horizontal slab projecting from the lower part of the monument.

As dusk fell Dr Borchhardt and his photographer appeared, dusty from a hot day on the acropolis. After washing and quenching their thirst in a spring near the dig-house they invited us to supper. For the night we were offered a choice of accommodation either in a tent on the acropolis-hill or in one of the beach-huts which Dr Borchhardt had rented for the season in Finike; unadventurously we decided on the latter quarters.

While the meal was being prepared by Ali, the Turkish owner of the house, and his long-suffering wife—he keeps another up in the yaila, we were told—our German friends took us up to the flat roof of the building for drinks. Reclining on old mattresses round a low table, we must have looked very like figures in an ancient banqueting-scene. The sun had set behind the deep blue wall of the Alaja Dağ in the west, which stood out against a lemon yellow sky. The rocky acropolis-hill above us still retained an afterglow of purple. From the dark groves and water-meadows around the house rose a breath of freshness, carrying with it a scent of citrus fruit. Sudden raucous shouts and wild snatches of song from the Yürük encampment on the hillside interrupted the distant chorus of frogs.

The local brandy seemed potent after a day without food, but a pilaf flavoured with pine-kernels and spices and a dish of beans mixed with fried minced meat soon restored us; and while Dr Borchhardt filled and refilled our glasses with red wine, we made plans for a meeting in Antalya with our German friends in a few days' time.

Finally our host got into his minibus to guide us through the night to our sleeping-quarters. Familiar with the road, he dashed ahead, while we lurched laboriously round holes and corners, occasionally catching an ever more distant reflection of his headlights sweeping over an alien nightscape. In Finike we found him waiting by a bridge, across which we reached a wide expanse of beach and the concrete box allotted to us.

City-walls and theatre of Limyra from the acropolis

20

THE ACROPOLIS OF LIMYRA

Wᴇ were up at dawn. The stillness outside was absolute. Even the sea beyond the pale sweep of the sandy bay scarcely moved. In the east a waxing streak of pink outlined the silhouette of the Chelidonian headland, while the higher reaches of the Alaja Dağ in the west began to be touched by the rays of the sun which was still hidden from view below the horizon. It seemed sacrilege to shatter such peace with the noise of our engine, but we had to reach the top of the acropolis before the sun became too fierce.

At the dig-house we joined the boy with the water-donkey who was to guide us up to the heroön. We passed some scattered black tents and exchanged greetings with the women and children who had begun to stir. Colourful tent-bags and striped rugs were being shaken out, and the pig-tails of reluct-ant, wild-eyed little girls were being plaited for the day. On the lower slopes of the hill the Yürük men have appropriated uncultivated land, and narrow terraces of poor soil show traces of stubble, while west of the theatre a few young olives struggle to survive.

We zig-zagged higher and higher in the wake of the donkey over the cleft and eroded scarp to which tufts of euphorbia and thistles cling tenaciously. On the skyline above our heads we caught an occasional glimpse of a moving figure beyond the parapet of the heroön-terrace. Work was already in full swing.

The temple-tomb of Limyra was of roughly the same size as the Nereid Monument of Xanthos and obviously inspired by it. But its position was far more spectacular. Sited on the southernmost tip of the acropolis rock, it over-looked the entire coastal plain and the sea. It was built from the limestone blocks cut from the mountain-side to create the platform on which it stands and a stairway, also carved from the living rock, leads down from its base to the edge of the precipice, a feature which must greatly have increased the apparent height of the monument. Enough of the masonry has survived to make a reconstruction of the building possible, a work which was being carried out with great skill under taxing conditions.

The base on which the tomb was raised is typically Lycian containing a burial chamber, but the tomb itself, which had a porch of four columns both in front and behind, is clearly modelled on the Temple of Athena Nike on the Acropolis of Athens, a building of the late 5th century B.C.; and the

columns, which are in the form of draped girls or Caryatids, imitate the
famous Caryatids of the south porch of the Erechtheum at Athens, a part of
the building which shelters the tomb of the mythical King Kekrops. The
pose of the Limyra maidens is stiffer than that of their Athenian prototypes,
their drapery more cumbersome, and their hair covered by a veil and twisted
into rigid, rope-like tresses. In their block-like massiveness they recall the
earliest-known female architectural supporting-figure, the basalt goddess in
the entrance of the temple-palace of Tell Halaf in northern Mesopotamia.
On their heavy wrists they wear bracelets terminating in lions' heads, a
typically Achaemenid form of jewellery. In one hand they hold a libation-
bowl and in the other a rhyton or ceremonial vessel, ending in the forepart

The heroön on the acropolis of Limyra

of a winged animal, a form derived from Asiatic prototypes and adapted for the cult of the dead in Greek and Lycian art.

Persian influence is also manifest in the figured frieze which decorated the long sides of the chamber of the heroön. Relatively well-preserved slabs show a procession of foot-soldiers and horsemen accompanying a chariot, perhaps that of the owner of the tomb. To the east side belongs a particularly beautiful slab carved with a group of five horsemen with strikingly individualized features riding abreast. Two of them are characterized as Persians by the tiara, the soft cap with lappets which cover the nape of the neck and are wrapped round the chin. The others are Greeks or Lycians, one wearing a helmet with cheek-pieces, another a cap, and the third a petasos, the flat Greek travelling-hat. Not only do the riders differ in their clothes, but their faces are deliberately varied to show that they beyong to ethnically different types; and the breeds of their horses are also differentiated. The intention was presumably to prove that many divers nationalities paid homage to the ruler.

Of the roof of the heroön fragments of the sima or gutter with spouts in the form of lions' heads are still preserved. The pediment and the corners of the roof were surmounted by acroterial figures. Though fragmentary and much weathered, these were being pieced together and are now housed in the Museum of Antalya. The central group was composed of a figure of Perseus hurrying over the prostrate body of the Gorgo Medusa, whose severed head he holds up triumphantly. The running figures of lightly-clad girls which formed the corner-acroteria are probably Medusa's sisters in vain pursuit of the hero. They are clearly copied from the windswept girls of the Nereid Monument of Xanthos, though slightly simplified, since the local limestone does not take the same high finish as marble.

According to Greek myth, Perseus was the father of Perses, who gave his name to the Persians when he became their king. In crowning his tomb with a figure of Perseus, the dynast may have intended to remind his Persian overlords that their race was once ruled by a king of Greek descent.

Behind the heroön the mountain rises further to form an elongated ridge joined by a col to the main massif of the Tocak Dağ to the north. It was occupied by a palace and a fortress, of which only scanty traces are still visible. The architect surveying the acropolis showed us the remains of scarped walls, the foundations of towers and a gate with well-preserved jambs and the cuttings for a lock. Among the confusion of tumbled masonry some conical blocks with a rounded top have been identified as merlons from the battlements. The fortress of Limyra must have looked exactly like the crenellated cities carved on the smaller battle-frieze of the Nereid Monument and on the friezes from the heroön at Gjölbashi-Trysa.

On our way back to the heroön we passed an elongated stone pedestal which may have supported statues and, further on, a group of enigmatic cuttings in low outcrops of rock. Rectangular holes with slightly bevelled edges hol-

A caryatid from the heroön at Limyra

Antiphellos. The Hellenistic theatre and the island of Castellorizo

Rock-cut containers on the acropolis of Limyra

lowed from rough cubes of living rock, these cuttings are thought to be fire-altars. That many elements of Persian 'cult and court-ritual penetrated into Lycian culture is not surprising in view of more than 200 years of Persian domination of Asia Minor, and the elevated site would be suitable as an emplacement for an Achaemenid fire-altar. But the shape of these cuttings differs from the fire-altars at Naksh-i-Rustem and Taq-i-Bostan in Iran, and perhaps these stone troughs with sunken rims (which look as if they were meant to hold stone slabs as lids) might have served as *ostothekai*, containers for the bones of incinerated dead.

The view from the terrace of the heroön is stupendous. King Perikle's choice of this site for his acropolis was eminently strategic: impregnable to assault from below, it commanded the entire plain from the Chelidonian headland to Finike, its harbour-town. This fertile crescent, which is watered by three rivers, is one of the largest stretches of easily cultivable land in Lycia and must have provided the economic basis for the king's power.

At the foot of the acropolis-hill the pale conch of the theatre and the cogged line of the Roman city-wall look minute, like toys abandoned by a child. Amid swamps in the as yet unexcavated part of the Roman city lie the remains of a funerary monument of Caius Caesar. A son of Agrippa and Julia, he was born in 20 B.C. and adopted by the Emperor Augustus three years later; but while campaigning in Armenia in A.D. 4 he received a wound, from which he died at Limyra on his way back to Italy. A bishop's palace and a church have been identified in the ruins of the Byzantine city which adjoined the Roman city on the east; but excavation here is hampered by the marshiness of the ground.

21

ELMALI AND ANTALYA

T HE road to Elmalı follows the course of the Arycandus upstream through a
landscape of alpine beauty. In the shingly river-bed clumps of oleander
form islands of shiny dark green and pink between rills of grey mountain
water. Tall pines climb up the steep slopes on either side. Their scent, mixed
with that of thyme and other herbs, drifted in through the open window:
pungent essences distilled by the heat.

Traffic was heavier here than on the lonely Lycian coast and consisted
mainly of timber-lorries; as of old, wood from these mountains is an important export article. Until the end of the 19th century the small, scattered tribe
of the Tahtajis (Woodcutters) lived in these forests. Quite distinct from the
Yürüks in their language, their round, felt-covered huts, their long hair and
the head-dress of their unveiled women, they were reputed to be devil-
worshippers by their Turkish neighbours.

Winding up through pine-covered defiles and round outcrops of rock of
cyclopean size, we reached a considerable height. At one point we made out
grey walls of ashlar masonry high up on the right of the road, the remains of
the ancient city of Arycanda dominating the valley on its steep cliff. Beyond
the zone of tall forests came alpine meadows with patches of agriculture and
stunted trees, then another pass, after which the landscape suddenly changed
completely: we had entered the region known as Milyas in antiquity.

Huge barren hills enclose flat valleys which gradually open out into dreary
plains of grey clayey soil, former lake-bottoms which are now partly drained
and cultivated. Skirting the Awlan Göl, we noticed bulldozers and draglines
at work on a drainage-canal in the distance, their bright orange paint the only
cheerful note in a subdued range of colours: fawn hills, grey earth and silvery-
yellow stubble.

Elmalı, the town of the apples, lies up against the foot of the Elmalı Dağ
on the northern edge of a plain. Ringed by orchards and poplars, it is a
prosperous little country-town with a mosque of the 15th century, a wide
asphalted main-street, pleasant public gardens and a good lokanta. An
American archaeological mission has its headquarters here during the excavation season; and its work has produced a great deal of new information about
the early history of the region. Among the mission's most exciting discoveries
are two frescoed tumulus-tombs, one at Kızılbel overlooking the lake of

Elmalı and the other on the Karaburun ridge to the west of the Korkuteli road between the villages of Semayük and Bayindir.

The frescoes, which date from the late 6th and early 5th centuries B.C., were badly damaged when found and are now in course of restoration. They are of absorbing interest since hardly any painted Greek tomb-chambers of contemporary date have survived; the only paintings of this period which can be compared with them in quality and size are those in the Etruscan tombs of Tarquinia and Chiusi. Like the Etruscan paintings, the newly-found frescoes illustrate scenes of banqueting and hunting but the range of subjects represented in the Kızılbel tumulus alone is far greater than that of any single Etruscan tomb, while the mixture of local Lycian, East Greek, Persian and Oriental elements in the Karaburun tumulus makes this discovery one of the most fascinating for the study of Anatolia's role as a link between East and West.

Continuing northwards across the plateau, we joined the dusty inland road from Fethiye to Antalya and shortly afterwards descended into the plain of Korkuteli, watered by a river and green with flourishing orchards.

Beyond the little town the road is asphalted and driving a pleasure, though we had to slow down frequently to nose our way past families of villagers returning with their flocks from the high-lying yailas to the plains. The increasingly wooded slopes beside the road were dotted with colourful encampments: mothers squatting over improvised fires to prepare food, children playing, men tinkering with the harness of horses and camels or adjusting loads of bedding and household-utensils. Their carts were of two types: some shallow and rectangular, their sides brightly painted with village-scenes and floral patterns, others with tall, rounded hoods of canvas resembling waggons on Etruscan and Roman reliefs.

The road winds down in sweeping, well-engineered curves hugging the bluffs and spurs of the craggy mountainside and threading its way round the northern echelons of the chains which tower like gigantic ramparts above the whole length of the eastern Lycian coast. Some 37 km east of Korkuteli, half-way down a narrow gorge, the road is crossed by a well-preserved ancient wall of ashlar masonry reinforced by towers on its west side. A gate in the wall proves that the ancient road also passed through it at this point. The fortification comes to a sudden end on the far side of the hill to the north, and it is difficult to say what its purpose was. The fact that it faces west might suggest that it was a frontier defence of Pamphylia, but in view of its closeness to Termessus it is perhaps more likely to have been built by that city. As Freya Stark has pointed out, it makes no sense militarily. Termessus was perched far above the road on a well-walled height and needed no lower defences. Professor Bean has plausibly conjectured that it was a customs barrier which allowed the Termessians to levy toll on all passing traffic. A little to the east of this puzzling wall a new motor track on the right of the road leads up to Termessus amidst its wooded hills.

Leaving exploration of the ancient city for another day, we continued to-wards Antalya and presently reached level stretches of well-tended forests, where picnic sites, fire warnings and hotel advertisements announced the proximity of a big city. Suddenly the line of trees on the right of the road receded and we found ourselves on the southern edge of a plateau looking out on a panorama of striking grandeur. The Pamphylian plain, which descends from the Taurus range towards the Mediterranean in a series of low terraces of calcareous deposits, meets the barrier of the Lycian mountains here at its westernmost end, forming the great arc of the bay of Antalya. The sea was already darkening in the shadow of the rocky peaks.

On the last of the Pamphylian limestone-terraces, surrounding a nearly circular harbour, lies Antalya, the ancient Attaleia, founded about 158 B.C. by King Attalus II of Pergamum. Approaching Antalya from the north, no signs of its antiquity are noticeable. The road plunges over the edge of the plateau beside a waterfall tamed within its concrete bed, and becomes a dual carriage-way of grandiose proportions leading due south towards the box-like modern buildings of the outskirts. In the low cliff face overlooking the road a number of caves are cut, but their crudely shaped entrances may be comparatively recent, the work of shepherds or squatters.

Hoping to find a room in the Perge Oteli we turned east towards the Karaalı Parkı, skirting the ancient city-walls. The original Hellenistic masonry has survived in the lowest courses of some of the square towers; but the upper parts are largely Byzantine work of the 10th century A.D. with later Seljuk additions. The stone used throughout is the porous local lime-stone, which has weathered to a mellow brown. When Captain Beaufort visited Antalya in 1811, the circuit of the walls was still complete, but it has since been reduced to less than half its original length.

As the Perge Oteli was full, we made for the Büyük (Grand) Hotel in the western part of the town. It is splendidly situated on a terrace looking down on the harbour and adjoins a large square dominated by a gigantic bronze figure of Atatürk on a prancing horse.

While we were still settling into our balconied room, darkness fell. On the large esplanade below the hotel garden the citizens of Antalya were enjoying the evening air and sipping their glasses of tea or raki.

Dining on the terrace of the Büyük Hotel a little later, we were entertained by the scene, visible through the open doors of the dining-room, of a cir-cumcision party within. A local family and their numerous well-to-do friends were celebrating the occasion with a lavish dinner, while the young boy in whose honour the feast took place surveyed the scene from a huge polished bed placed in a corner of the room. Still looking pale and shocked and dressed in a white shirt with a red sash and a silver embroidered pill-box cap on his head, the boy had been carried in by his father and deposited on the bed. He revived visibly as all the guests made much of him and presents began to pile up on the beautifully embroidered bed-spread. Meanwhile a band in white ties and tails played a mixture of Turkish tunes and American jazz. A group of British tourists who had just flown in were clearly mystified by the whole performance. 'You don't mean it's done by a priest,' exclaimed a matron in a low-cut, floral-print dress on learning from the maître d'hôtel what was involved, 'surely they ought to get a surgeon!'

22

OLD ANTALYA

THE museum of Antalya was until recently housed in an attractive group of old Turkish buildings occupying two terraces near the clock tower in the centre of the town. On the upper level stands a small türbe or Islamic tomb, of almost abstract beauty. No ornament disturbs the purity of its lines and proportions. A white-washed octagon with a pale-buff roof in the form of a tent, it has uncluttered, faceted surfaces composed like those of a crystal.

A staircase festooned with purple bougainvillaea leads down to the lower level, where a magnificent minaret thrusts skywards. Above a polygonal base inset with panels of tiles rises the powerful, fluted shaft of pinkish brick, spangled with small pieces of bluish-green fayence and crowned by a balcony and a conical top. Built in the early 13th century A.D. by the sultan Alâ-et-Tin Kaykobat, it is known as the Yivli Minare, the fluted minaret. Its vigour and simplicity is characteristic of Alâ-et-Tin's architecture, as can be seen at Konya, where his large mosque is preserved on the flank of the mound which was once the old Seljuk citadel. Next to the minaret at Antalya is a mosque converted from a late 13th-century church. Pleasant though it is with its white-washed walls and six brown tiled domes, it lacks the spare, bold lines of early Seljuk art. On the same terrace as the minaret and mosque are the ruins of an ancient Medresse or Koranic school with a richly-carved portal.

The mosque served as the archaeological museum of Antalya, but a larger museum has since been opened in a beautiful position on the western out-skirts of the town. New finds from all over Pamphylia and Lycia are being brought in almost daily, and the collection of sculptures is among the most important in Turkey.

Just as we had finished looking at the museum, we found that Dr Borchhardt had arrived in his minibus with a new load of fragmentary sculp-ture from the heroön at Limyra. Spreading the various shapeless-looking lumps of broken drapery and limbs out on the museum terrace, he and his restorer began sorting out the joins and sticking them together with a special adhesive. An elderly museum warder observed the operation with lively interest, not, as it turned out, from any love of archaeology, but because he hoped to get his broken denture mended with the same miraculous medium.

Leaving our German friends to their task, we climbed arduously to the top of the Yivli Minare, from where there is an unobstructed view of the whole expanse of the eastern flank of the Lycian mountains, from the southern-most point of the Chelidonian headland, indistinct in a haze of heat and distance, to the peaks towering above Termessus in the north. On a head land half-way between these two extremities lie the ruins of Phaselis and, not far to the south of Phaselis, those of Olympus. It was through the mountain-chains behind these cities that Alexander the Great marched from Lycia to Pamphylia by a bold route which Freya Stark has retraced in modern times.

From the foot of the museum terrace the snuff-coloured roofs of the old city of Antalya slope gradually downwards towards the small rock-bound harbour. We strolled along the cobbled streets, lined by quiet gardens and remnants of the ancient ramparts isolated between groups of houses. A surprising number of the typical Turkish wooden houses have survived. The central window of the projecting upper storey is usually latticed by a bulging, pear-shaped screen, which serves as an observation post from which the ladies can discreetly observe life in the street below. The upper storeys of houses on opposite sides of the narrow alleyways often almost meet, and neighbours can speak to each other without raising their voices.

There are also stone-built houses with elegantly decorated ogival door-ways, flanked by pilasters carved in low relief. The concave eaves of the wooden roofs are sometimes stuccoed and painted with a blue and white arabesque, sometimes left unstuccoed, so that their beautiful joinery, which often forms a rosette or star, is exposed. Through doors left ajar we caught an occasional glimpse of tree-shaded courtyards surrounded by wooden galleries.

In the midst of the labyrinth of lanes to the north-east of the harbour stands the Kesik Minare or truncated minaret, beside the ruins of a Christian basilica of the 5th century A.D. which was sacred to the Panaghia, the Virgin Mary. It is built of a rather gloomy brown stone and has window-frames of white marble carved in lacy patterns and a marble doorway which it may have inherited from a pagan temple. The minaret was added in the 13th century, when the church was converted into a mosque. Time has now overtaken the Moslem use of the building, too, and only a stump of the minaret survives, while the desolate interior of the basilica is full of rubbish and rank weeds.

Passing through a gap in the ramparts which tower above the almost circular harbour basin, we descended a steep flight of steps overhung by ancient plane-trees and reached the quayside. Small fishing-boats were tied up there and rust-coloured nets spread out to be mended. Next to a little mosque a fountain splashed and old men with bubbling water-pipes sat in placid contemplation. The only biggish boat in the harbour was an elderly freighter waiting to load a cargo of Lycian timber, a great oval raft of reddish

Roman Mausoleum at Antalya

pine-trunks which was being slowly but surely manoeuvred towards it by a single hefty oarsman in a rowing-boat.

High up on the cliffs to the east of the harbour stands an important monument of the Roman period known as the Hıdırlık Kulesı, which has been mistakenly identified as an ancient light-house and even as a Venetian tower. It is, in fact, a mausoleum, the shape of which recalls the tomb of Caecilia Metella on the Via Appia south of Rome and, to cite an even more famous example, that of the Emperor Hadrian, the Castel Sant'Angelo in Rome itself. Built from the local golden-brown stone, the Hıdırlık Kulesı consists of a massive square base with an entrance at ground level flanked by twelve fasces or bundles of rods tied round an axe, which show that it must have been the tomb of a Roman magistrate. The tomb-chamber itself was accessible from a door at a lower level on the northern side, now half hidden by rubbish. The upper, drum-like part of the building has a window above the main entrance, and gutter-spouts projecting at the four points of the compass serve to drain the crenellated flat roof. The parapet of poor masonry which now crowns the tomb is a later addition.

Another imposing, though much restored monument of the Roman period is the Gate of Hadrian, erected on the occasion of the emperor's visit to Attaleia in A.D. 130. Framed by two massive square towers of the Hellenistic city-wall, this elegant triple arch is a purely decorative and honorific structure, without any defensive purpose. Four Corinthian marble columns on detached pedestals flank the coffered arches which are of equal height. The entablature is ornamented with a frieze and floral scrolls and the gutter or sima above it is carved with palmettes and lions' heads. Originally the arch had an upper storey, which bore the Greek dedication to Hadrian in gilt bronze letters. The letters spelling the name of the emperor's adoptive father Trajan came to light in 1882 near the gateway and are now in the Ashmolean Museum, Oxford.

23

TERMESSUS

THE morning we had chosen to drive to Termessus turned out to be misty. It was the equinox, a date liable to bring a change of weather. Occasionally the sun broke through, revealing glimpses of the sea, only to be swallowed up again by fast-moving swirls of a luminous haze. Up in the wooded mountains near Termessus the sky was a little clearer than by the sea, but drifts of cloud kept rolling over the crest of Güllük Dağ (Mount Solymos) from the south and hung picturesquely between the crags and pines, until a puff of fresh wind dispersed them.

The new motor-track which branches off the Korkuteli road to the left skirts the northern flank of Mount Solymos and, winding past an isolated ancient tower, comes to an end on a level stretch of ground between steep hills. The absolute quiet of this glen was broken only by the occasional twitter of a bird and by the scurrying of numerous squirrels. Here holm-oaks, creepers and thick undergrowth form an almost impenetrable jungle covering the slopes which are full of tombs. The city itself, equally overgrown, lies higher up on a saddle of a lesser peak of Güllük Dağ. It was discovered by Schönborn in 1841 and identified as Termessus by Spratt and Forbes who visited it in the following year. No adequate plan of the city exists and a modern survey is urgently required. Few sites look a more promising field for the excavator.

Termessus was a Pisidian city, but no inscriptions in the native language have survived, a fact which suggests that it was Hellenized relatively early. Of the large number of Greek inscriptions found there the oldest date from the 2nd century B.C., but the majority are comparatively late and cover the period when Termessus was 'a friend and ally of the Roman people'. In some of these inscriptions the inhabitants refer to themselves as Solymi. Homer already knew the Solymi (*Iliad* 6. 184 f.) as the warlike neighbours of the Lycians, against whom Bellerophon was sent to fight by King Iobates of Lycia after overcoming the Chimaera. The geographer Strabo first identified the inhabitants of Termessus with the Solymi on the grounds that their city lay under Mount Solymos and their main divinity was Zeus Solymeus. The name Termessus has the same root as Termilae, an ancient name for the Lycians.

We began our visit by investigating the remains of the propylon or monu-

Propylon at Termessus

mental gateway to a ruined Hadrianic temple dominating the little plain where we had left our car. A tall flight of steps, now a cascade of architectural fragments, led up to the doorway of the propylon, the frame of which, crowned by a richly-carved lintel, still stands intact. Round about lie numerous column drums and blocks of ashlar masonry, sufficient, one would guess, for the building to be reconstructed.

As we were walking uphill towards the city, a couple of small boys emerged from the undergrowth, and one of them offered to guide us to the theatre. They were the sons of the local yangın bekçi, the Forestry Commission fire-warden, whose cottage is the only modern habitation on the site. After a steep climb up the narrowing valley we came upon a stretch of the handsome lower city-wall with a projecting tower on the hillside above us on the left. Just beyond the tower a round shield is carved in the beautifully finished masonry, an emblem not infrequently found on Pisidian and Pamphylian fortifications and perhaps representing actual shields taken as booty from the enemy and hung up on the walls in celebration of victory. Originally the wall must have formed an angle shortly above this point and turned to span the valley in a north-westerly direction, thus blocking the only practicable route up from the north. In view of the city's virtually impregnable position one can understand why Alexander the Great decided to abandon his brief siege of Termessus (333 B.C.)

As we climbed on, the upper city wall appeared, a bastion shoring up the main part of the town, which is situated on a slope between the rocky ridges to east and west. Just below it on the left of the path lie the huge overgrown ruins of a gymnasium.

The theatre of Termessus and Mount Solymos

On a saddle above and to the south of the gymnasium and just within the city-wall stands the Hellenistic theatre. According to the Greek pattern, its well-preserved cavea exceeds a semicircle. It faces east and had its main entrance through an arched door in the centre of the back wall with a stairway leading down to the lower seats. The stage building, originally detached from the auditorium, was altered in the Roman period and joined to the right-hand part of the cavea to provide additional seats. The back wall of the stage still survives with its five doors intact; in its Roman phase it was faced with free-standing columns on pedestals, of which the central pair, flanking the tallest doorway, were spirally fluted, while the rest were plain. The low stage front also had five doors, which opened into the orchestra, and was decorated with carved shields set in square panels. On the return of each of the projecting side-walls of the stage building a cuirass was carved in relief.

Beyond the back wall of the stage the pine-skirted twin peaks of Mount Solymos were, at the time of our visit, alternately veiled and revealed by fast moving mist, as in some Chinese painting. To the right of Solymos a precipitous gorge leading down to the Pamphylian plain afforded occasional glimpses of distant Antalya and the sea.

South-west of the theatre lies a square building preserved to a height of some ten metres, its upper part decorated on three sides with shallow Doric pilasters. The south and east walls were pierced by windows, eleven in all. The interior, which was originally roofed all over and panelled with coloured marble, is now a ruin filled with rubble and vegetation. But faint traces of curved rows of seats can still be made out and suggest that this impressive structure was either a council-chamber or, more probably, an odeum or hall for musical and poetry performances. Names inscribed on the outside of the north wall are those of victors not, as one might expect on such a building, in musical contests, but in sporting events, such as horse and foot races and wrestling, which must have taken place in the nearby gymnasium or in the city's stadium, of which no trace has been found so far.

Directly next to the odeum is a small but exquisitely built temple which may have been dedicated to the city's patron-god, Zeus Solymeus. Only its walls are preserved and a bench for statues at the back of the chamber.

The main temple of Zeus must have been situated to the west of this shrine, where a huge mass of architectural debris covers the slope. Here the Austrian archaeologists who surveyed Termessus in 1884 found fragments of reliefs showing Zeus and other divinities battling with giants and a circular base carved with a sacrificial scene.

A further group of temples stands on a platform projecting south from the odeum. One of them, whose doorway is still intact and flanked by statue-bases, was, according to an inscription above the lintel, sacred to Artemis and built at the expense of a lady called Aurelia Armasta. It dates from the early 3rd century A.D.

Nearby are the foundations of a larger Ionic temple which must also have been dedicated to Artemis, to judge from two reliefs with representations of the myth of Iphigeneia which were found among the debris at its east end. Next to Zeus Solymeus, the goddess was obviously the Termessians most important divinity.

Further west, beyond the market square, stands another small shrine, which is almost completely overgrown. Built in the Corinthian order on a high platform with four columns on the front, it was accessible by a staircase on the east side. One well-preserved corner of the building emerges above the jungle-like vegetation. Its dedication is unknown.

From here we reached the market-place, once bordered by irregularly aligned columnar porticoes which have collapsed in earthquakes and under the thrust of roots. At its south-west end a large natural outcrop of rock has been carved into a funerary monument for some local hero. The actual sepulchre, which was recessed in the back of a rock-cut platform, was approached by a stairway flanked by curved seats. In the smooth upright face of the platform are three irregular niches, perhaps for votive offerings. The name of the hero to whom this intriguing monument belonged is not preserved. The two men whose names are carved in large slanting letters on another side of the rock must have been buried somewhere nearby.

Rock-cut relief in the Tomb of Alketas at Termessus

Under the once paved, but now grass-covered market-square the ground sounds hollow, and in its centre we came upon a line of circular openings, the mouths of five large subterranean cisterns. The supply of spring water for the town was clearly insufficient and had to be supplemented by the collection of rain water.

Leaving the market-place we passed between the corners of two ruined porticoes, the western built by King Attalos II of Pergamum, whom the Termessians seem to have helped in his war against the Selgians, the northern erected by a local benefactor named Osbaras.

Our young guide next led us to a spring hidden among debris on the north side of the market-square —the only spring now existing in the city—and hauled up several draughts of excellent water in a jam-tin on a string. But he obviously intended this to be his final bene-faction, and when we asked him to show us the tomb of Alketas, the most important of all the funerary monuments of Termessus, he obstinately de-clared that we had seen everything and began to trot off downhill.

We set off, no less determinedly, in the opposite direction, towards the foot of the rampart of cliffs shielding the town on the north-west, where we knew that the rock-tombs must be situated. The thickets of tangled trees and creepers appeared almost impenetrable, but fortunately our guide changed his mind and presently caught up with us again.

Emerging from the vegetation, we found ourselves in front of a large two-sided recess at the foot of the sheer, strongly stratified cliff-face. On the left-hand wall of the recess a roughly-shaped arch frames the life-size figure of a galloping horseman in relief. The hind legs of the horse are missing, broken away with a huge block split off by an earthquake. The rider, who sits on a saddle-cloth, wears a leather corselet and a cloak which flies out behind him. His right hand is raised to throw a spear, which must originally have been rendered in paint. His head, which seems to have been helmeted, is badly mutilated. At a lower level on the same panel of rock are carved a round shield and behind it a sword with a handle in the form of a bird's head. Above the shield appears a crested helmet and below it a pair of greaves.

The central feature of the right-hand wall of the recess is a sarcophagus in the form of a funerary couch with legs decorated with palmettes. Behind the couch, which is badly damaged, a kind of baldachin is carved in low relief. Above it soars a heraldic eagle with wings spread and a snake in its talons. To the left of the sarcophagus an *ostotheke*, or container for bones and ashes, is hewn from the rock, its front decorated with a small doorway in relief. To the right are the remains of three containers, also cut from the living rock, and perhaps intended for liquid offerings. Two of them are rectangular boxes with lions' heads carved on their fronts, and the right-hand box bears in addition two small figures, perhaps Dionysos and Aphrodite, on its left side. Between these two containers and at a lower level is a large mixing-bowl, the side of which is broken away; a low table for offerings stands in front of the sarcophagus.

Sadly ruined though it is, the tomb is of great historical interest. It is almost certainly the funerary monument which, according to Diodorus, the young warriors of Termessus made for the Macedonian cavalry leader Alketas, the brother of Alexander the Great's general Perdikkas.

Betrayed by the elder citizens of the town, where he had taken refuge from Antigonos in 319 B.C., Alketas committed suicide rather than fall into the hands of his enemy. His body, which the elders surrendered to Antigonos, was shamefully treated and left unburied, until the loyal young Termessians recovered it and gave it a splendid burial.

Numerous other tombs are carved into the rock-face on this western side of the city, but with the exception of two of Lycian type none is as early as that of Alketas. The large south-western and northern cemeteries of Termessus are of the Roman period and consist mainly of sarcophagi. Some of the sarcophagi are cut from the living rock; others are carved from detached blocks and set, singly or in groups, on stepped platforms or within small funerary temples or *aediculae*. Their decoration frequently includes the motif of a shield in front of crossed lances. Most of these lichen-covered sarcophagi now gape empty, their lids tumbled in desolate confusion, like the tombs in a medieval representation of the Last Judgement.

Antalya. The Yivli Minare

24

FROM PAMPHYLIA INTO PHRYGIA

WE had spent a week in Pamphylia, the ample 'Land of all Tribes', and visited the sites of Perge, Aspendos and Side. These splendid and spacious ancient cities with their vast theatres, stadia, colonnaded streets and monumental fountains are a world apart from the sparer mountain-cities of Lycia and Pisidia, and in driving north again from Antalya, we felt we were returning to familiar territory from a digression.

Leaving the Korkuteli road on our left, we took the main road north to Isparta. Soon the tall pine forests gave way to wide sweeps of stubble and straggling villages. The monotony of sagging telephone lines beside the road was broken by pairs of bee-eaters perched on the wires. At the foot of the bleached hills to the west occasional sudden hollows of green marked the spots where springs gush forth from the limestone. Further on ponds and a placid little lake with floating water-lilies refreshed the eye. Just before the road begins to climb up into the mountains, an old Seljuk han, foursquare and rugged, appears on the right, a resting-place for travellers on their way to the interior.

In spectacular hairpin-bends we wound to the top of the Çubuk Boğazı Pass to find ourselves once more in the harsh beauty of the barren hills of the plateau, which owe their colour to cloud-shadows rather than vegetation. Small harvested plains and valleys lap round the foot-hills. From time to time we overtook a lumbering agricultural cart of archaic design drawn by a yoke of oxen. The upper part of the vehicle is constructed like the ribs of a boat and can be taken off the wheel-base; we saw one such turned upside down with a blanket over it to shade a baby from the sun, while the parents worked in the fields. The wheels are solid discs of wood, composed of six pieces arranged in two concentric circles round the hub.

An occasional patch of strong yellow flecked the dusty fields, the harvest of corn on the cob. Near the small town of Aglasun women were crouching round heaps of cobs which they were stripping, while beside them an old man stood winnowing. The sun caught the shining corns which he threw up into the air and transformed them into a rain of gold, the chaff blowing away in a dull cloud.

Aglasun, whose name preserves that of the ancient city of Sagalassus, lies at the foot of a craggy mountain where plentiful springs have created an oasis of fruit trees, walnuts and poplars. In the village square, presided over by the usual bronze effigy of Atatürk, some pieces of ancient sculpture have been assembled round the knotty trunk of an ancient plane tree: a veiled female figure, the fragment of a columnar sarcophagus, a stele carved with a bunch of grapes and a couple of big marble bowls on fluted stands, their upper parts decorated with swags of fruit suspended from staring tragic masks. This form of funerary urn seems to be peculiar to Sagalassus, for we have met it nowhere else. (A small number of them are preserved in the museum of Burdur.)

Pisidian urns at Aglasun

Like Termessus, the city was a flourishing settlement of fiercely independent and warlike Pisidians. Alexander the Great on his way north to
Gordium in 333 B.C. overcame the Sagalassians after a hard uphill battle;
and these tough mountain warriors were again defeated some 140 years later,
by the Roman consul Cnaeus Manlius Vulso. But in the unshaken calm of
imperial times, the Pax Romana, Sagalassus became a prosperous city with
two theatres and market-places and temples dedicated to Apollo Clarios and
to the Emperor Antoninus Pius. Though agriculture and commerce had
now replaced warfare and the mercenary calling on which the Pisidians had
long based their economy, their passion for the military life must have been
deep-rooted, for even in the Roman period their tombs abound in representations of shields, helmets and swords.

The scattered ruins of the city lie high on a steep mountain-shelf to the
north of modern Aglasun; but we disappointed an army of small boys who
were anxious to act as guides and pointed uphill with eager shouts of 'Tiyatro';
we had no time for the climb since our stage for the night was Pamukkale,
the ancient Hierapolis, in Phrygia.

We passed through Isparta, caught a glimpse of the Lake of Burdur, silvery-
blue in its mountain-girt depression, and, just short of Dinar, reached the
great road leading west towards Denizli and Izmir, along which we had
travelled ten years ago. The hamlets here have undergone a great change; the
low mud-brick huts with flat roofs, almost merging with the landscape in
their subdued dun colour, have been replaced by neat white-washed, red-
roofed houses, petrol stations and great hoardings advertising 'Hand-made
carpets straight from the producer'.

But the Acı Gölü, the Bitter Lake, one of the salt-lakes typical of the
plateau, was just as we remembered it: the leaden surface, ringed by sparkling
crusts of salt, sustains no life on its shores. Eerily calm, the water mirrors
the dark scarp of the Yan Dağ behind it, the foot of which is stained a deep
russet by ferriferous rock. Euphorbia and low grey, salt-loving plants cover
the stony ground sloping down towards the lake from the road.

As we drove on, the afternoon sun began to turn the widening, richly-
modelled valley of the upper Lycus into a Claude-like landscape of gold and
blue. In a dip beside the road just short of Denizli lies the mellow stone
square of a fine 13th-century caravanseray, the Ak Han, its façade distinguished by an arched entrance-gate and corner-towers. Shortly afterwards
we turned north on a wide new asphalt road, which cuts through cotton
fields dotted with brightly-dressed women, their sack-like aprons bulging
with the last pickings of the harvest. A clamorous array of advertisements
for hotels in Pamukkale warned us that we might not find the site as un-
touched and lovely as we remembered it.

25

HIERAPOLIS REVISITED

A DAZZLINGLY white terrace of calcareous deposits on the slope of the Çal Dağ to the north of the Lycus valley makes the city conspicuous from afar. The lime-bearing thermal springs which rise on the plateau of Hierapolis have raised the ground-level of the site considerably since antiquity, incrusting the remains of the ancient city and of a medieval castle with limestone deposits and continuously extending the width of the ledge on which the ruins are situated. Fanning out from a central spring along countless, ever growing natural aqueducts, the water has trickled over the edge of the mountain shelf forming cascades of shell-like basins spilling over into chalky stalactites. A principal channel, so long accreted that it has become a kind of sloping causeway, descends from the centre of the plateau's edge to the valley below, watering the fields and gardens of the modern village. Pamukkale means Cotton Castle in Turkish and refers to the medieval fortress perched on the brink of the terrace and engulfed by the white deposits.

The modern road leads up to the site cutting straight across the lime-incrusted scarp to reach a depressing waste-land of parking lots, leaning electricity and telegraph poles, advertisements and garish souvenir booths: the lonely ancient city has become a tourist resort with half a dozen sprawling new motels, most of which incorporate one or more of the natural limestone basins in their gardens of hibiscus and oleander and also use the warm blue mineral water to fill their swimming pools. The hotels are pleasant and comfortable enough, but one cannot help regretting the destruction of the former magical solitude of the site.

Lying on the line of the great strategic road from the Mediterranean coast to Central Anatolia, Hierapolis was founded during the second quarter of the 2nd century B.C., probably by King Eumenes II of Pergamum; but of the Hellenistic city little has survived. Together with the rest of the Pergamene kingdom it was bequeathed to Rome by King Attalos III who died in 133 B.C.; and it is to the Roman period that most of the city's existing ruins belong. About A.D. 60, in the reign of the Emperor Nero, a violent earthquake—the worst of a whole series which had visited the city—almost totally destroyed it and most of the surviving buildings are post-Neronian.

The ruins were first scientifically explored by German archaeologists in 1887, and extensive excavations have been carried out in recent years by an

The arch of Domitian at Hierapolis

Italian mission.

Most of the public buildings of the city (which was planned on a regular grid-pattern) were aligned on a long colonnaded street which runs from north to south, roughly parallel to the edge of the plateau, and terminated at each end in a monumental gateway, of which only the northern is well preserved. Built from the local brownish limestone, which resembles travertine, the gate has three arches of equal height and is flanked by two circular towers. Like the arch of Hadrian at Antalya it originally had an upper storey. An inscription, of which fragments have survived, records that it was dedicated to the emperor Domitian in A.D. 84–85 by the proconsul Frontinus.

Recent excavations in the vicinity of the gate have revealed the remains of a large tomb, which backed on to the western tower and has been reconstructed by the Italian archaeologists. It is an elegant cubic building with a door of marble imitating wooden construction, a pilaster at each corner and a Doric frieze with rosettes between the triglyphs. According to an inscription the tomb belonged to a widely travelled merchant named Flavius Zeuxis. On the lime-incrusted scarp of the plateau in front of the monument a number of other tombs have been engulfed by the deposits of the calcareous streams.

Approaching the edge over the hollow-sounding chalky ground to inspect a small house-shaped tomb, we found it imprisoned to half its height by a series of shallow super-imposed natural basins. The warm water brimming over their scalloped rims dispersed down the hillside, slowly petrifying the lower parts of the oleander bushes which cover the slope.

The main necropolis of the city lies along an extension of the colonnaded street leading north. This cemetery is of remarkable extent and contains a fascinating variety of tombs which have yielded numerous inscriptions throwing light on the social and economic life of the citizens.

Passing the imposing ruins of a large vaulted structure with three arches, originally baths but later converted into a Christian basilica, one enters a maze of sepulchres; all were broken into and robbed in antiquity. The apocalyptic jumble of gaping sarcophagi, scattered lids and toppled tombs which we remembered from our previous visit has been cleared up in recent years. There are house-like tombs with flat roofs; temple-shaped tombs with finely-carved mock doorways and decorated pediments; sarcophagi placed, singly or in groups on stone platforms or on tall pedestals; tumuli on circular stone bases, containing rectangular chambers with stone benches round three sides, the mounds crowned by phallic tomb-markers; and a peculiar barrel-vaulted type of tomb roofed with massive stone slabs laid lengthwise. The two latter types may still belong to the earliest, Hellenistic, period of the town. The circular tumuli bear a striking resemblance to the older Etruscan tumuli at Cerveteri, the barrel-vaulted tombs to the so-called Tanella di Pitagora in the plain beneath Cortona.

Still an attractive place today, the necropolis must have been even more agreeable in antiquity. As we learn from inscriptions discovered here, many of the individual tombs were surrounded by gardens, and others were annually decorated with wreaths paid for from funds held by official trustees. Some of the funerary monuments incorporate stone benches in their façades on which mourners could sit and draw comfort from the contemplation of flowers and plants which symbolized the eternal renewal of life. Other inscriptions mention a guild of gardeners and lend substance to the fame which the gardens and vineyards of Hierapolis, watered by its numerous streams, enjoyed in antiquity.

An unusual monument of a later period has recently been excavated on the hillside to the north-east of the city, its elevated site approached by a wide staircase. It is the 'Martyrium' of St Philip the Apostle, who spent his last days at Hierapolis. Built in the early 5th century A.D., it consists of an octagonal structure originally covered by a dome and set within a square of cells for pilgrims. In the colonnaded central hall, where commemorative services seem to have been conducted, a stepped semicircular bench for the clergy and the site of a lectern have been identified.

We had chosen to revisit the necropolis first, as the city was still crowded by the tourists who are brought up by fleets of buses and usually limit their sightseeing to the more spectacular monuments in the vicinity of their hotels. With the approach of the evening, however, we made our way south along the colonnaded street in comparative solitude. The low sun transformed the site into the magical landscape of a Pompeian fresco with ochre-coloured buildings casting long mauve shadows.

South of the triple gate of Domitian a stretch of the colonnaded street has

Tomb at Hierapolis

been partly excavated, revealing the underlying drainage-system and remains of earlier tombs. Lining the street are the lowest courses or foundations of spacious houses of the Roman period. The excavated area comes to an end at a Byzantine gate, which indicates by its position the extent to which the city was reduced in its decline.

Further along the street on its east side are the ruins of a large nymphaeum. A high rear wall and two projecting side walls surround a rectangular water-basin, accessible by a flight of steps in front. The monument was originally richly decorated with carved architectural members framing the five niches still preserved in the walls. The water was piped into the basin through a hole in the central recess of the rear wall.

To the west of the colonnaded street and a short distance below the Nymphaeum lies the Sacred Pool, which is now profanely enclosed by a motel and serves as its swimming-pool. Through the clear warm mineral water shimmer the foundations of a portico which lined the pool in the Roman period. Fluted column drums of marble and blocks of the entablature lie scattered at the bottom of the lime-incrusted basin.

In antiquity the most famous natural phenomenon of Hierapolis, apart from its therapeutic waters, was the Plutonium, an underground stream from which deadly vapours issued through a cleft in the rock. According to Strabo, Cassius Dio and other ancient writers, the noxious gases were capable of killing bulls and smaller creatures brought within the enclosure which surrounded the orifice in the hillside. Because of its underground nature and its lethal properties, the spot was considered the preserve of Pluto, the god of the Underworld. Until recently the location of the Plutonium was a mystery, since the site had become completely buried by thick layers of lime deposits; but it was discovered by the Italian excavators when they cleared the remains of the temple of Apollo which lies to the south-east of the Nymphaeum and is connected to it by a large colonnaded courtyard in the Doric order. The podium of this temple abuts at its rear on to a rocky shelf in which, immediately to the south of the podium, was revealed an opening with a fluted archivolt above giving access to a paved subterranean chamber. Within this chamber a strong stream runs in a natural fissure in the rock, emitting a sharp-smelling gas, probably carbon-dioxide, which acts as an irritant on eyes and throat and kills small creatures breathing it in its concentrated form on the bottom of the cave.

Higher up the hillside behind the Plutonium lies the Roman Theatre, one of the best preserved buildings of Hierapolis. In accordance with the Greek tradition the orchestra is circular and the large auditorium, which rises to a height of about 50 rows of seats, slightly exceeds a semicircle in plan. In the centre a box was reserved for important spectators, a semicircular recess with a curved stone seat supported on lions' paws and a footstool carved beneath it. It is probable that masonry from an earlier, Hellenistic theatre which was situated some distance to the north of Hierapolis has been re-used for the construction of the cavea.

The stage still stands almost complete, but its rear wall, the originally richly-carved scaenae frons, has partly collapsed and is in course of restoration. It had the normal five doors and, in addition, arched windows above. The fine decorative carvings of the stage building include reliefs with scenes from the life of Dionysus, the god of wine and the drama, the goddess Artemis on her chariot, figures of fleeing Niobids, religious processions and a sacrifice to the image of the Diana of the Ephesians. The emperor Septimius Severus and his family surrounded by allegorical figures were represented on a relief which adorned the upper part of the scaenae frons, an indication that this part of the theatre was erected in his reign (A.D. 193–211).

The grand view from the upper rows of the auditorium across the plateau and the valley of the Lycus to the snow-capped massif of Salbakos and Kadmos must always have provided a rival spectacle to that on the stage.

Another particularly well-preserved group of buildings is the large complex of baths and a palaestra or sportsground situated on the western edge of the plateau near the point where the modern road comes up from the valley. Some of the huge vaults of the bath-buildings constructed from massive blocks of the porous local limestone have survived intact, and small holes in the surface of the walls indicate that they were once incrusted with marble slabs held in position by metal pins.

One of the barrel-vaulted halls facing the edge of the plateau serves as a repository for the most vulnerable pieces of sculpture from the site, including a number carved with figures in a competent style which recalls that of Aphrodisias, a city to the south of Hierapolis renowned for its marble workers.

Among the rugs and embroideries offered for sale in the souvenir booths near the baths we noticed one or two fine old kelims, tempting reminders of the age-old local tradition of textile manufacture. Inscriptions found at Hierapolis have furnished evidence for the existence of trade-guilds of wool-washers, dyers and weavers. Instead of the rare and expensive purple dye extracted from the murex shell, the city's dyers employed a vegetable dye fixed with the help of the hot water of the local springs, which proved an effective and cheaper substitute. A large Jewish community appears to have contributed to the success of this ancient textile industry.

26

NYSA

WEST of Denizli near Sarayköy the Lycus joins the Maeander, whose
wide upper valley, enriched by fertile soil washed down from the steep
mountain ranges flanking it, is one vast orchard of olives, figs, apricots,
oranges and lemons with crops of vegetables flourishing in their shade. In
the village of Sultanhissar we turned off the main road to the right to drive
up into the foothills of the Aydin Mountains. Cleft and fragmented by countless torrents into wildly picturesque conical peaks and serrated ridges, these
south-facing slopes are almost as fertile as the Maeander-valley they overlook. A good new asphalt road leads up to the ruins of the city of Nysa ad
Maeandrum or Carian Nysa, as it was called to distinguish it from the
many other ancient cities of the same name.

According to the Greek geographer Strabo, Nysa was created by uniting
three independent earlier settlements founded by the Spartan brothers
Athymbrus, Athymbrades and Hydrelus, whose names they bore. It is likely
that the new city, which was at first called Athymbra, was founded in the
3rd century B.C. by one of the successors of Alexander the Great, probably
Antiochus I Soter, the son of Seleucus; it was renamed Nysa at some time
in the early 2nd century B.C., perhaps in honour of a Seleucid princess of
that name.

Strabo, who was born about 63 B.C. in Amasia in Pontus (the modern
Amasya near Samsun), has left us a description of the site of Nysa, which he
knew well, having studied rhetoric and grammar there under Aristodemus.
When speaking of the lay-out of the city, he seems to have been surveying
it from a point above the theatre on the southern slope of Mount Messogis;
and so it was to the theatre that we first made our way on arriving at the
ruins.

The large cavea, cut into the hillside, has recently been cleared and is
comparatively well preserved with 48 rows of seats. Like the theatre of
Hierapolis and many other Roman theatres of Asia Minor, it follows Greek
prototypes in slightly exceeding the semicircle in plan. The stage building
had the usual five doors in its back wall and a richly decorated front; but
much of it has collapsed and awaits further excavation. What gives the
theatre of Nysa its unique character is the grove of ancient olive trees which
cling to the limestone steps of the auditorium at various levels. Their branches

moving in a slight breeze, they reminded us of the last eager spectators in an emptying theatre who, by their persistent clapping, hope to extort yet another appearance of the actors.

From the uppermost rows of the cavea the view south strikes one both by its grandeur and by its close correspondence to Strabo's description. Beyond the ruined stage building the hillside is riven by a deep ravine. This precipitous gully is formed by the torrent of Tekkeçikdere, which rises high up among the peaks of Mount Messogis. Rushing in a southerly direction past the east side of the theatre, it changes its course to the west in front of it and then resumes its southward run down to the Maeander valley. This, then, is the torrential stream which, Strabo says, split Nysa into a kind of double city by its ravine. But whereas now its bed, covered by scrub and crumbling ruins, is fully exposed up to the point where it disappears in a notch over the southern edge of the plateau, in antiquity it was largely concealed by an amphitheatre with thirty rows of seats supported on enormous vaulted substructions spanning the ravine. Strabo's two cities were, in fact, joined by this daring architecture, underneath which the stream ran hidden, its waters available when the arena had to be flooded for staging naval battles or other aquatic performances.

An equally remarkable feat of engineering was the erection of two bridges and the building of a huge tunnel about 150 metres long, which covered the course of the river where it changed direction and thus created a large piazza between the theatre and the northern end of the amphitheatre. The western end of the tunnel has been worn away by erosion and the entrance to it is now visible a little to the south of the stage building.

The other public buildings mentioned by Strabo can almost all be identified, though they underwent considerable alterations after his day. The modern approach-road skirts the long side of a large rectangle on the western side of the ravine, presumably Strabo's gymnasium. In the late 3rd century A.D. it was surrounded by an arcaded colonnade, of which the German archaeologists who explored Nysa in 1907 and 1909 found only scanty traces, most of the masonry having been removed when the railway was built through the Maeander valley.

To the south of the gymnasium, arches and walls of poor workmanship mark the site of a bathing establishment, to judge from the large quantity of water pipes leading towards them. The original lay-out of the establishment has been obscured by a Byzantine church installed within the remains, which now bear the name Kâtip Ören.

Just north of the gymnasium, in an olive grove on a higher level, stands an interesting rectangular building which Strabo does not mention, no doubt because it did not yet exist in his day. This ruin has been identified as a library because its construction closely resembles that of the library of Celsus at Ephesus. Though not nearly as well preserved as the latter, it would

certainly repay excavation and restoration.

At present its ground floor is almost completely filled by rubble. Only the short side walls and the niched inner walls of the building, which may originally have risen to a height of three storeys, emerge between the trees. The south façade, which contained the entrance, has completely disappeared, but in the poorly-preserved north wall the remains of window openings have been traced. The shallow niches on the inside of the double east and west walls were once fitted with shelves for the storage of manuscript scrolls.

Though sadly ruinous, it is still a most attractive building, human in scale and conjuring up an atmosphere of cloistered and studious calm within its grey walls.

Returning to the theatre, we made our way to the eastern side of the ravine where, Strabo tells us, the agora and gerontikon of Nysa were situated. The great level space of the agora or market place is now a harvested field dotted with ancient olives; except for a few column drums nothing remains of the porticoes which originally surrounded it. But the German excavators found that the east and north sides of the square were once lined by two-aisled Ionic colonnades, while on the south and west sides there were single Doric porticoes.

The gerontikon or council-chamber of the elders is situated close to the north-west angle of the agora. It, too, has been altered and rebuilt several times. What Strabo saw must have been a late Hellenistic structure which was perhaps unroofed. Its present massive enclosure walls, which probably date from the late 2nd century A.D., are largely composed of rough and irregular re-used masonry which must originally have been concealed by a veneer of coloured marble, of which many fragments have been found by the excavators. The interior of the building, to which three doors in the south side gave access, contains a handsome semicircle of limestone seats, twelve rows high, with five radial staircases. The floor facing the seats is paved with regular stone slabs. On the north side of the chamber there was an ante-room, accessible from the outside through four pairs of columns of unusual elliptical shape.

Sounds of rushing water and of rustling leaves are the only noises to be heard at Nysa, which for the moment still combines an unspoilt natural setting with easy accessibility. The upper regions of Mount Messogis to the north of the city were famed in antiquity for their fruitfulness and their wine, in particular that of a village fittingly named Aroma. They are still covered by rich vegetation.

Still higher up, just below the trachyte peaks of Kızıl Kaya, lies the isolated grassy plain described by Strabo as the Nysaean leimōn. According to him, this meadow was a gathering place of the people of Nysa and their neighbours. A deep abyss connected it with Acharaca, a village to the south-west of Nysa, which was the site of a renowned sanctuary of the gods of the underworld and where there was a cave known as the Charonium, in which miraculous cures were effected by incubation. The Nysaean leimōn, a meadow of alpine beauty, seems to have remained a numinous place throughout the centuries and still shelters the tomb of an Islamic saint under secular oak trees.

To the west of Nysa and divided from it by deep torrent-beds lies the city's necropolis, distinguished by its long rows of vaulted burial-chambers, often two storeys high, which line the road to Acharaca.

27

CLAROS AND NOTIUM

SOUTH of Izmir extends the great plain of Cumaovası, rimmed by wooded hills which form a chain along the northern coast of the bay of Kuşadası. Through this range of hills several rivers have worked their way south to the sea, one of them the ancient Ales or Halesus in whose valley the sites of Claros and Notium are situated.

The river rises in the territory of Colophon, a city famed in antiquity for its wealth and, like Sybaris, notorious for its extravagance. The produce of Colophon's rich agricultural land was exported through its harbour town Notium on the mouth of the Halesus. The Colophonians' luxurious habits led them to forget their original prowess in war—their cavalry and navy had been renowned—and the men who cared more for purple robes and costly scent than for arms fell an easy prey to the assaults of the Lydian king Gyges in the 7th century B.C. and of the Persians in the 6th. Like many other cities of Asia Minor, Colophon joined the Delian confederacy which Athens founded after the defeat of the Persians in 479 B.C., but a pro-Persian party seized power in the city later in the century. In Hellenistic times the city suffered during the wars between Alexander the Great's successors, being destroyed in 299 B.C. by Lysimachus who settled the survivors in his newly-founded city of Ephesus. Although Colophon was rebuilt on its original site after Lysimachus' death, it never regained its old prosperity, its trade having been captured by the expanding Ephesus with its richer hinterland. The harbour town of Notium was now called New Colophon or Colophon-by-the-Sea, while the original Colophon was distinguished as the Old City.

The ruins of both Colophon and Notium were first identified by German scholars in 1886, and the remains of Colophon were excavated by American archaeologists in 1922. The city covered an extensive area of three adjacent hills and a valley traversed by small streams. But its scanty ruins, which include traces of houses, streets, remains of a temple of Demeter Anteia and of Hellenistic city walls, are overgrown by dense pine-forests and difficult to locate. A resin known as colophonia was already being extracted from the local pines in antiquity.

The most famous site in the territory of Colophon was the Oracle and Temple of Apollo at Claros in the lower valley of the Halesus about 1 mile from the mouth of the river at Notium. This oracular sanctuary flourished particularly during the Hellenistic and Roman period, but it is connected in myth with prophetesses and seers of a far earlier time. The Sibyl Herophile is said to have come to Claros before the Trojan War; and later the prophetess Manto fled here from Thebes and married the Greek leader of Cretan settlers who had driven the original Carian inhabitants from the place. Manto gave birth to Mopsus, who himself became a famous seer and the mythical founder of several cities in Pamphylia. Although Sibyls seem to have been prominent in the legendary early history of the site, during the historical existence of the oracle, divination was practised exclusively by male priests.

From the Roman historian Tacitus we learn that the priest, having heard no more than the names of the enquirers, went down into a cave at night and drank there from a secret spring whereupon he was able to divine the questions which his clients had in mind and uttered responses to them. 'A pool in the cave of Clarian Apollo' is also mentioned by Pliny, and the search for it was long bedevilled by the assumption that the cave must be a natural one outside the temple. Until comparatively recently it was identified with a grotto high up in a cliff face in a side valley of the Halesus despite the inaccessibility of the spot. In 1950, however, the French excavators of Claros finally solved the problem of the oracle's location. After clearing the sanctuary of the deep alluvial deposits which had entirely covered it—an excavation of great difficulty owing to the constant necessity of pumping away ground water—they found that the Temple of Apollo contained subterranean chambers obviously adapted for divination.

We approached Claros over a dust track which forks off the good asphalt road leading from Izmir straight to the coast at Notium. The level valley bottom, sheltered between low, scrub covered hills, was partly cultivated with the area of the excavation left fallow—a maze of hollows, trenches and deposits of soil on which weeds and spindly trees have taken hold. In recent years the water table has risen again and covered the foundations of the newly revealed buildings, but luckily for us an exceptionally dry summer had drained the site completely. Despite the present neglect of the excavation, the general lay-out of the sanctuary is easily intelligible.

A Doric propylon or monumental gateway with four columns at the front and two at the back, marked the entrance to the temple-precinct, which included a sacred grove. In antiquity most visitors to Claros arrived by sea and, having landed at Notium, approached the sanctuary from the south, on which side the propylon is situated. Its surviving columns are covered with inscriptions, mainly dating from Roman imperial times and naming deputations from widely scattered cities in Asia Minor and eastern Europe who had come to consult the oracle. Also inscribed here are the names of young people who sang in choirs to honour Apollo on festive occasions. The columns of the Propylon were the only vestige of Claros still remaining visible above the swampy alluvial deposits in the 19th century, and were thought to be part

Left leg of the over life-size marble figure of Apollo at Claros

of the Temple of Apollo until the true nature of the building was discovered by the French excavation. At present it lies at the bottom of a hollow, shaded by sparse trees.

On the west side of the Propylon a colonnaded hall provided space for business transactions, and on the east side stands a well-preserved semicircular exedra, a curved bench on which tired visitors could rest before approaching the Temple.

A sacred way led north from the Propylon to the eastern front of the Temple of Apollo, flanked on either side by small monuments and votive statues and dedications, the bases of which have in part survived. Of the temple only the foundations and the platform remain, the colonnade and the chamber having been destroyed by earthquake and subsequent stone-robbing. It was a Doric peripteros standing on a platform five steps high and having eleven columns on the long sides and six at each end. From the form of the columns and capitals, some of which are still lying on the site, the temple appears to have been built in the late 4th century B.C. and probably replaced an earlier shrine. But the construction must have stretched over a long period, for an inscription on the architrave records that the colonnade was only completed in the reign of the emperor Hadrian (A.D. 117–38). On the east side the four topmost steps of the temple-platform are entirely covered with inscribed names, partly of visitors who had consulted the oracle, and partly of the members of choirs.

Entered through a deep colonnaded porch at its east end, the temple-chamber contained a group of three cult-images, gigantic fragments of which have survived on the spot. On the evidence of coins of Colophon, Apollo Clarios, the principal god of the sanctuary, was represented seated between two goddesses, presumably his mother Leto and his sister Artemis. The huge fragments lying about haphazardly on the pavement slabs of the cella include pieces of one male and two draped female figures. The largest preserved piece, which is about 3·50 metres long, must be the left leg of the statue of Apollo, who sat, with only his lower limbs draped, holding a laurel branch in his right hand and resting his left arm on a lyre. The statues, which must have been carved in the early Hellenistic period, are of great importance by virtue of their quality and size. Not many original cult-figures of the late 4th century B.C. have come down to us, and one hopes that these precious fragments will soon be rescued from the deterioration which in their present exposed state they will inevitably suffer.

The oracular chamber and well were found at the western end of the temple in the foundations of the cella. Arched ribs spanning two adjacent basement rooms, too low for a man to stand upright, served to support the pavement of the cella above. These cave-like rooms were reached by two corridors of blue marble entered at the eastern end of the temple and meeting and diverging again with a confusing number of right-angle turns. In the first chamber, which was fitted with marble benches between the springs of the arched ribs, an omphalos was discovered, a domed stone symbolizing the navel of the earth at Delphi and sacred to Apollo. Here the *thespiodos* or composer of the oracular responses in verse must have waited with the scribes who wrote them down, while the priests penetrated through a narrow passage into the adyton, the inner chamber, where he drank the prophetic water. The excavators found a rectangular well surrounded by a high parapet to the left of the entrance of this inner sanctum, which lay directly underneath the statue of Apollo. This unique and complex lay-out fits so perfectly Tacitus' description of the priest descending into a cave to drink from a sacred spring that there can no longer be any doubt that this is in fact the oracle of which he and other ancient writers speak.

To the east of the temple a large altar has been excavated with two separate sacrificial slabs: one for Apollo, the other for Dionysus, whose worship here, as at Delphi, was associated with that of the principal god of the sanctuary. A stone sun-dial, dedicated to Dionysus, stands nearby.

To the north-west of the main temple a smaller Ionic temple and an altar have been found. An archaic female statue discovered on the spot bears a dedication by one Timonax, son of Theodorus, to Artemis Claria, to whom the temple must have belonged. Nothing survives of the cult-statue itself, but it appears on local coins as an unpleasing, stiff image, resembling the Ephesian Artemis in general shape.

That the sanctuary was in use already in the 6th century B.C. is proved not only by Timonax' votive gift, but by other archaic votive figures, including one of a man holding a sacrificial calf, now in the museum at Izmir. Among the dedications which have remained at Claros, particular historical interest attaches to one inscribed on a stone pillar south of the altar of Apollo, which mentions Cicero's brother, Quintus Tullius Cicero, governor of the province of Asia (61–59 B.C.). A little to the south of this pillar stands a handsome stone chair, its sides carved with floral scrolls and the arm-rests shaped like winged serpents.

The ruins of Notium lie on a conspicuous rise on the left bank of the Halesus, where it debouches into the wide bay of Kuşadası, about a mile to the south of Claros. According to Herodotus, Notium was Aeolian, the southernmost of the original twelve Aeolian cities, and surrounded by Ionians. Its situation on an easily defensible height, by the mouth of a river which provided not only a harbour but communication with the agricultural hinterland, combined military with economic advantages. The rich Ionian Colophon depended on Notium as an outlet for its produce and as a naval base; and in the days of Colophon's early greatness Notium, too, must have prospered. When both cities fell to the Persians, their decline was shared. The Peloponnesian War brought a division between the two cities which was to last until the conquest of Alexander the Great: factional strife within the cities resulted in a pro-Persian party taking over at Colophon, while Notium, for a while divided between a pro-Persian and a pro-Athenian party, eventually re-established its allegiance to Athens. In Hellenistic and Roman times Notium fared better than her formerly predominant partner and finally assumed the very name of Colophon.

The beach at Notium, now all too easily accessible from Izmir, is threatened by development; and the clean sweep of sand between the flanking hills is already disfigured by a couple of restaurants and a cluster of newly-constructed holiday villas. Leaving the car near them, we made our way along a ditch of brackish water—a vestige, perhaps, of the ancient harbour—which runs back inland between the precipitous western side of the city and harvested fields where mandrake plants still cradled their yellow fruit within frilly-leaved

Carved stone chair at Claros

rosettes. At the head of the ditch a side-valley opens to the east, isolating the double eminence of Notium from the mountain ridge which flanks the Halesus valley and in whose south-western slope the city's necropolis is situated.

Turning seawards again, we climbed the steep ascent to the ancient city. Of the Hellenistic walls which once surrounded it, extensive stretches still survive on the south-west and north-east. The wall, which has projecting square towers at regular intervals, is constructed of ashlar masonry, but shows signs of later repairs at several points. The circuit hugs the hill near the top of the slope and closely follows the outlines of its two lofty promontories connected by a col.

On top of the westernmost height are the scanty remains of a small temple dedicated to Athena Polias, which was excavated by a French archaeological mission in 1921. A Corinthian building of the time of the emperor Hadrian (A.D. 117–38), the temple stood on a platform of three steps and was decorated with a frieze of laurel garlands suspended from bulls' heads. It had an altar in front of its east end and was set, curiously off-centre, within a rectangular Doric portico. Only the foundations and a few column drums are now visible among the low scrub.

Towards the centre of the plateau the foundations can be traced of a square market place, from the eastern side of which projected a small chamber with stepped seats running round three sides of the interior, an arrangement reminiscent of the council chamber of Priene and suggesting that here, too, the building was a bouleuterion.

Further east, beyond the col, a small theatre nestles in the hillside facing west. It has not yet been excavated and is much overgrown, but enough of it can be seen to infer that it was probably built in the Hellenistic period and remodelled in Roman imperial times. To the south-east of the theatre and close to the city-wall, which is comparatively well preserved here, a second market place was situated, but hardly anything of it survives.

However insignificant the remains of Notium may be, the site itself is strikingly beautiful and affords splendid views. We certainly did not regret our climb. Seen from the highest point of the hill, the two promontories of Notium ride the sea like twin ships sailing into the gulf of Ephesus. Beyond the wide gulf—roughened now into silver by the meltemi—the headland of Kuşadası and the long rocky ridge of Mycale interlock with the wooded hillsides of Samos, coulisse behind coulisse in ever hazier shades of blue. This is where modern Greece and Asia almost come into physical contact; and from our vantage point the overlapping of cape and island created the comforting illusion of a geographical continuity reflecting the cultural unity always tangible in the ancient remains. Further to the south, hidden behind this vast panorama, lie Caria and Lycia, the Land of the Chimaera, the goal of our journey to which we hope to return one day.

GLOSSARY

Acropolis—Citadel

Acroterium—Figures or ornaments at the apex and the outer angles of a pediment

Adyton—The inner or most holy room of a temple

Agora—A public square or market place

Anta—Pilaster forming the end of the lateral wall of a temple cella

Apse—A semicircular annex to a building or a recess in a wall

Architrave—The horizontal element of stone or timber spanning the interval between two columns

Ashlar—Regular masonry of squared stones laid in horizontal courses with vertical joints

Basilica—An oblong rectangular building, usually with a nave and lateral aisles, which in Roman times served as exchange and court of law

Bouleuterion—The Greek council-chamber

Capital—The topmost member of a column or pilaster

Caryatid—Female figure replacing a column to support an entablature

Cavea—The auditorium of a theatre

Cella—The chamber of a temple

Cornice—The upper member of a classical entablature

Dentils—Decorative motif in the bed-mould of a cornice or occupying the place of a frieze, derived from the rectangular ends of joists

Entablature—The horizontal superstructure carried by a colonnade, usually divided into three parts: the architrave, the frieze and the cornice

Exedra—Semicircular or rectangular recess

Frieze—The middle member of an entablature, usually decorated with relief-sculpture

Gerontikon—Council-chamber of the elders of a Greek city

Hellenistic—The historical period between Alexander the Great (*d.* 321 B.C.) and Julius Caesar (*d.* 44 B.C.)

Heroön—A small shrine or chapel for the worship of the dead or of demi-gods

Insula—Tenement or apartment house or block in a city of rectangular plan

Lintel—A horizontal beam across a door or window-opening

Merlons—The crenellations of a fortress wall

Metope—The panel, plain or decorated, between the triglyphs of a Doric entablature

Nymphaeum—Originally a chamber, sometimes a grotto, with running water sacred to the nymphs; later any public fountain with rich architectural decoration

Odeum—Small roofed theatre for concerts or lectures

Omphalos—'Navel'. The navel of the world, a cone-shaped stone in the sanctuary of Apollo at Delphi and, by imitation, in other sanctuaries of Apollo

Orchestra—Originally the circular 'dancing floor' in a Greek theatre; in the Roman theatre the semicircular space in front of the stage

Orthostat—Upright slab of stone used in the lower part of a wall

Palaestra—Exercise ground

Parodos—Lateral entrance to the orchestra of a theatre

Pediment—Triangular gabled end of a ridged roof, including the tympanum and the raking cornice above it

Peripteros—Temple with a continuous outer ring of columns

Podium—The platform of a temple, normally with a moulding at the bottom and the top

Propylaeum or *propylon*—Entrance-gate building to a temple-precinct or monumental building

Proscaenium—The stage of a theatre in front of the stage building

Scaena—Stage building of a Roman theatre

Scaenae frons—The façade of the stage building which constitutes the backdrop of the stage

Sima—Crowning moulding of a cornice which was originally the gutter of the building

Stadium—A race-course

Stele—Upright slab of stone, usually carved

Temenos—Sacred enclosure or precinct

Triglyph—Projecting member of the Doric frieze consisting of a block with three vertical grooves and situated between the metopes

SELECT BIBLIOGRAPHY

(Listed in chronological order of publication)

R. Chandler. *Travels in Asia Minor 1764–1765*. Edited and abridged by Edith Clay. British Museum, London, 1971.

Count Choiseul Gouffier. *Voyage pittoresque de la Grèce*. Vol. I. Paris, 1782.

L. Mayer. *Views in the Ottoman Empire, chiefly in Karamania, a part of Asia Minor hitherto unexplored*. London, 1803.

J. v. Hammer (v. Hammer Purgstall). *Topographische Ansichten gesammelt auf einer Reise in die Levante*. Wien, 1811.

F. Beaufort. *Karamania or a brief description of the coast of Asia Minor and of the remains of antiquity, 1811–1812*. London, 1818.

C. R. Cockerell. *Journal of Travels in Southern Europe and the Levant*. Edited by Samuel Pepys Cockerell. London, 1903.

R. Walpole. *Travels in various countries of the East*. London, 1820.

W. M. Leake. *Journal of a Tour of Asia Minor*. London, 1824.

C. Texier. *Description de l'Asie Mineure faite par l'ordre du Gouvernement Français de 1833 à 1837*. Paris, 1849.

C. Fellows. *A Journal written during an excursion in Asia Minor*. London, 1839.

Discoveries in Lycia. London, 1841.

T. A. B. Spratt and E. Forbes. *Travels in Lycia, Milyas and the Cibyratis*. 2 vols. London, 1847.

C. T. Newton. *Discoveries at Halicarnassus, Cnidus and Branchidae*. 2 vols. London, 1862.

O. Benndorf und G. Niemann. *Reisen in Lykien und Karien*. Wien, 1884.

E. Petersen und F. von Luschan. *Reisen im südwestlichen Kleinasien*. Wien, 1889.

Karl Graf Lanckorónski unter Mitwirkung von G. Niemann und E. Petersen. *Städte Pamphyliens und Pisidiens*. Wien, 1890.

O. Benndorf, G. Niemann. *Das Heroön von Gjölbashi–Trysa*. Wien, 1890.

E. Kalinka. *Bericht über zwei Reisen im südwestlichen Kleinasien. Denkschrift der Kaiserlichen Akademie der Wissenschaften in Wien XLV, 1*. 1890.

Tituli Asiae Minoris Vol. I. Tituli Lyciae lingua Lycia conscripti. Wien, 1901.

G. Humann. *Altertümer von Hierapolis*. Berlin, 1898.

W. v. Diest. *Nysa ad Maeandrum*. Berlin, 1913.

Th. Wiegand. *Der Latmos*. Berlin, 1913.

F. Eichler, *Die Reliefs des Heroön von Gjölbashi-Trysa*. Wien, 1950.

Freya Stark. *The Lycian Shore*. London, 1956.
   Alexander's Path. London, 1958.

J. M. Cook. *The Greeks in Ionia and the East*. London, 1962.

G. E. Bean. *Aegean Turkey*. London, 1966.
   Turkey's Southern Shore. London, 1968.
   Turkey beyond the Maeander. London, 1971.

P. Demargne. *Fouilles de Xanthos. Tome I. Les piliers funéraires*. Paris, 1958.

H. Metzger. *Fouilles de Xanthos. Tome II. L'acropole Lycienne*. Paris, 1963.

P. Coupel et P. Demargne. *Fouilles de Xanthos. Tome III. Le Monument des Nereides*. Paris, 1969.

W. Radt. *Siedlungen und Bauten auf der Halbinsel von Halikarnassos. Beiheft 3 der Istanbuler Mitteilungen*. 1970.

E. Akurgal. *Ancient Civilizations and ruins of Turkey*. Istanbul, 1970.

J. Borchhardt. *Myra*. Istanbuler Forschungen 30, 1974.

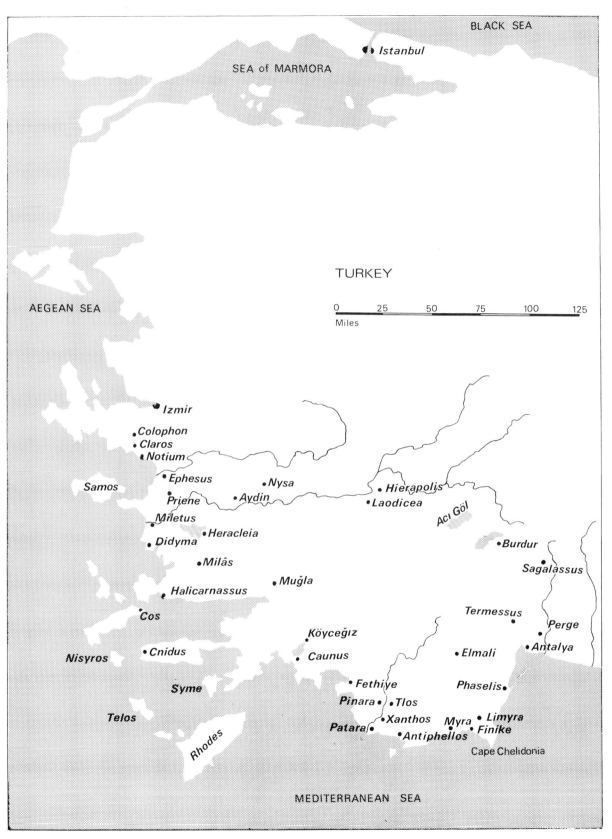

BLACK SEA

SEA of MARMORA

•) Istanbul

AEGEAN SEA

TURKEY

0   25   50   75   100   125
Miles

•Izmir

•Colophon
•Claros
•Notium

Samos

•Ephesus   •Nysa

•Priene   •Aydin

•Hierapolis
•Laodicea

Acı Göl

•Miletus

•Heracleia

•Didyma

•Milâs

•Burdur

Sagalassus

•Muğla

•Halicarnassus

•Cos

Nisyros

•Cnidus

Termessus

•Perge

•Antalya

Köyceğiz

•Caunus

•Elmali

Syme

Telos

•Fethiye

Phaselis

Pinara •   •Tlos

Rhodes

Patara •   •Xanthos

Myra   •Limyra

•Antiphellos   •Finike

Cape Chelidonia

MEDITERRANEAN SEA

Map of Western Turkey

Detail map of South-Western Turkey

Korkuteli •

PISIDIA

Güllük Dağ
Mount Solymos

Termessus •

Antalya
Attaleia

• Karataş-Semayük

*...*malı Dağ

• Elmalı

MILYAS

Podalia

Awlan Göl

Bashgöz Çay

Alağir Çay

Arycanda

Arycandus

Tahtaly Dağ
Phaselis •

Corydalla

Olympos

Limyra •

Demre
Çay

Myrus

Finike •

Gagae

jölbaşı

Trysa • Demre

Sura • *Myra*

• *Andriaka*

Cape Fineka

...riae

...owa

Cape Chelidonia

5   10   15   20
miles

INDEX